Karen + Anthony Flores

"The fragmentation and disintegration of the family is one of the saddest tragedies of our times. A solid, loving marriage is the first step to restoring the home. This book offers biblical and practical insights that can benefit anyone married one week or fifty years."

David Cook, President
International Bible College
San Antonio, Texas

"The principles taught in this book have been practiced and lived out in a great marriage. The power of Ruth's message comes from the depths of her commitment to Jesus Christ, and to those to whom she addresses them. This is the product of many years of research and practical experience."

Pastor Leonard Fox
Inland Christian Center Church
Colton, California

"In these times there can't be enough said on how to develop and maintain a "WOW Marriage." John and Ruth Bell are two of my heroes for a series of reasons, one of them being the fact that they have maintained a "WOW Marriage" before all of us who have had the privilege of being mentored by them. The principles shared in this book will be keys to opening up brand new dimensions of joy and fulfillment in our marriages.

"Thank you, Sister Bell, not only for writing these principles in a simple, understandable way, but also living them out before our eyes for as long as I can remember."

Marcos Witt, author, composer, president and founder of:
"Congreso De Adorades" (Worship Congresses)
"Canzion Productions" (Christian studios)
"Centro De Capacitaciones Y Dynamicas
Musicales" (School of Music),
Durango, Durango, Mexico

"This is a special book filled with warm, loving advice about the marriage relationship. Every chapter presents the easily-read true story of decades of a hands-on 'leaving, cleaving, and weaving' of two lives into a tapestry of love, hope, and commitment. We human beings have such finite minds, and sometimes godly precepts for faithful fidelity can seem far too abstract to hurting, frustrated husbands and wives. Ruth Bell has taken the principles of the wonders of a truly godly marriage and translated them into practical steps anyone can walk. I recommend that husbands, wives, fathers and mothers in-law, sons and daughters in-law all read this book. It will bless and encourage every one of them."

Rev. Liberty Savard
Author of *Shattering Your*
Strongholds and Breaking the Power

It's never too late to have a

WOW
Marriage

It's never too late to have a

WOW
Marriage

Ruth Bell

Bridge-Logos *Publishers*

North Brunswick, NJ

Unless otherwise indicated all Scripture quotations are from
the King James Version of the Bible.

It's Never Too Late To Have A WOW Marriage
by Ruth Bell
ISBN: 0-88270-741-8
Library of Congress Catalog Card Number: 97-73695
Copyright © 1997 by Ruth Esther Bell

Published by:
Bridge-Logos *Publishers*
North Brunswick Corporate Center
1300 Airport Road, Suite E
North Brunswick, NJ 08902

Dedication

To those who desire a wonderful, God-centered *WOW Marriage*

and who are willing to submit themselves to each other and to the principles of God's Word,

with thanksgiving in my heart for my beautiful *WOW Marriage* of fifty-plus years,

I lovingly dedicate these twelve principles with earnest prayers for your *WOW Marriage*.

Contents

Foreword

Seldom does one have the opportunity to glean from a book that provides a seat at the feet of one of the most fascinating Christian women this century has produced.

Seldom does one have the opportunity to be stirred by a book that has been drawn from a wealth of vast spiritual experience, spanning several decades of ministry from Japan before World War II to San Antonio in the 90's, with many "heart" stops in between.

Seldom does one have the opportunity to be challenged by a book that connects pivotal biblical truth with today's critical struggles in marriages, using generous helpings of real life situations to drive the truths home.

In my opinion *"It's Never Too Late To Have A WOW Marriage"* offers all of the above! For perhaps hundreds of women, men, and children, Ruth Bell over the years has become a matriarch—a cherished, experienced sister in Christ whom God has used to establish a direction for their lives. The principles in this book are the things she taught them.

There is rescue in these pages as she exposes lie after skillful lie the enemy often uses to paralyze marriages.

There is practical help for those starting out as well as those with many years of marriage who want to finish well.

There is humor—you cannot know Ruth Bell unless you experience her transparent wit. You will laugh as she honestly discloses her frustrations and her predicaments, and you will marvel at the "humanness" in her relationship with her pastor-husband, John, who is by the way, one of the godliest Christian gentlemen I have ever met. Ruth's conviction, and she delivers it well, is that, besides the individual believer's intimacy with the Lord Jesus, marriage in the power of the Holy Spirit should be the atmosphere for the greatest joy, and the context for the richest happiness to be found this side of heaven for a man and a woman. Thus she picked as her title *"It's Never Too Late To Have A WOW Marriage"*—and the title betrays her happy bias.

Dr. David Walker, Pastor
The Alamo City Baptist Church
San Antonio, Texas

1

Make Jesus Lord Of Your Future

*For I know him (Abraham), that he will command
... his household after him, and they shall keep the way
of the Lord .*

(Genesis 18:19)

It was our wedding night. We had just arrived at our hotel for our honeymoon. As we stepped into our lovely room on the fourth floor, he took me in his arms. Both of us were a bit nervous. We were now married—husband and wife. For two years we had dreamed of this day. Awesome!

It was late and we were very tired. Exhausted, we sat down on the couch, and discussed briefly who would take the first bath. At his insistence, I began to prepare.

He was twenty-one and I was nineteen; very young, and very innocent. We had met at Bible College, and were both virgins. He was a young minister, and I the daughter of missionaries.

I was born in Japan and lived there until I was fourteen: a life of security and protection. Mine was a wonderful Christ-filled family. My new husband was from the farm: his mother was a beautiful Christian but his dad was unsaved and frequently upset the family with his drinking and anger.

My bath was leisurely and long—three times he knocked gently on the door and asked if I was okay. Was I afraid to leave the bathroom? Not exactly, but it was sort of scary, being alone with this wonderful man, a man that I had loved for several years, had prayed for, had fasted with, had dreamed and planned with—now I was his wife. Wow!

As I sat in the tub, I asked myself, "Who is this Johnny Bell that I've married? What does the future hold for us together?" I thought I knew him well, but suddenly began to realize I hardly knew him at all.

What had attracted me to him was his honesty, his character, and his steadfastness, a trait that was missing in many of the young men I had dated in America. Most of all, the call of God on his life, and his devotion to the Lord and His Word had drawn me.

Another knock on the bathroom door. *I'd better stop daydreaming and get with it.* Hurriedly I dried and put on my beautiful negligee the youth group at church had given me. (I was glad it covered me completely as I exited the bathroom.)

I thought he would rush through his bath, but no, he was just as slow as I was. I sat on the couch reading my Bible, a habit my parents had instilled in me since early childhood.

When a young couple gets married, the habits of their childhood become very important. In fact, those habits often spell the difference between failure and success in the new relationship. Looking back now, I am grateful to my godly parents for the disciplines they spoke into my life, though admittedly, I wasn't fond of some of them at the time.

Finally the bathroom door opened, and out came this tall young man. I couldn't believe we were actually married. The dream of my whole life had come true. We belonged to each other forever!

My heart flipped and I jumped up and was enfolded into his beautiful embrace.

It was a long, tender moment. Not passionate, but gentle and warm. As I stood there in his arms, a sense of peace and security swept over me. Somehow, all the fear disappeared, and one of the verses sung at our wedding began humming in my heart: "Gone is the sorrow, gone doubt and fear, for you love me truly, truly dear." I felt overwhelmed by his love.

We sat on the couch and read the Bible together. Then he led me toward the bed and we got down on our knees, and arm in arm, we dedicated ourselves and our future to God, for whatever His design or plan might be. With his call into ministry and my background of the mission field, we were both vividly aware that our destiny would doubtless include heavy involvement with missions, possibly entailing sacrifice and hardships.

Though "the lordship of Jesus" has become a common phrase in recent years, in those days, I wasn't conscious of the concept at all. I was saved at my daddy's knee at age four and had served the Lord wholeheartedly all my life, but the lordship idea was unknown to me.

The first time I became aware of it was years later when I heard the song, "Jesus is Lord" at a Christian Businessmen's meeting at a hotel. That night, my spirit grabbed it. It melted me all over. I really related to it. However, God doesn't limit Himself to men's catch-phrases though He certainly uses them.

There by the bed, Johnny and I gave ourselves to God in a new and meaningful way. It was total commitment. But what was beautiful was that as we gave ourselves and our future to the Lord in this new dimension, we were also giving ourselves to each other in a new way. It was a moment I shall never forget, a prayer that even today blankets my spirit with tears as I recall it. It was as if a godly foundation was being established under our marriage.

That night, I gave my virginity to my new husband, and he gave himself to me. Though the world has made sex cheap and uses it for greed and entertainment, Christians should remember that true sex was not invented by Hollywood, nor for the pornographers, but by God. The Bible declares that *"Marriage is honorable in all, and the bed is undefiled; but whoremongers and adulterers God will judge"* (Hebrews 13:4).

All the next day, we couldn't stand to be even five inches apart. When we went out to eat or whatever we did, we had to feel the other real close. To sit across the table in a restaurant was too far removed. We had to sit side by side so we could touch each other every minute. It was truly a "one-flesh" experience, which continues even after fifty years.

I had wondered as a girl if marriage could be like this or if it would sort of start out this way, and end up in a cold routine. Thank God, if He is Lord it can continue with that glowing romance forever. The foundational key is, make Jesus Lord of everything, including your future—forever.

Life for us has been wonderful. The glow of our love has continued through storms and deserts as well as through beautiful gardens and mountains. God has always been there to protect, to provide, and teach us His ways.

Part of making Jesus Lord of your *WOW* marriage includes some basic principles that are important for young

4

newlyweds to not only be generally aware of, but to deliberately implement. I list some of them here:

1. Get involved in a good Bible church and be faithful to all of its services. Commit yourself to the pastor and the leadership. Give them the freedom to speak into your life, and if they correct you, take it joyfully. Be faithful with your tithing, and use your talents there. This is important.

2. Form the habit of a decent bed time. Many young couples stay up late and they are a wreck the next morning. They then rush off to work without breakfast or prayer together, and in this mad rush, they sometimes say unintended hurtful things that are never forgotten. Late nights on a regular basis can help to destroy a marriage. Plan a decent bed time and work toward it—say 10:30 P.M. or thereabouts.

3. Try to eat breakfast together. This is part of forming a "family" atmosphere in your new little home. Eating together is important. One of my college professors told us he read a statistic that said people who eat breakfast have the least amount of accidents, make the highest grades in school, and are among the few who don't have a weight problem. I like to think that there's a reason why God put our mouths in the front of our heads instead of in the back—it is for fellowship. And this fellowship is important before the couple separates for the day.

4. Form the "Family Devotions" habit from the beginning. Eating breakfast together not only adds to your "togetherness" at the start of your day, it also provides an opportunity for you to form the "Family Devotions" habit. From the beginning of our marriage, at the close of breakfast every day we have read a short passage of Scripture together, then prayed

together for the day, and said the Lord's Prayer in unison. This is a powerful way to start a new day. If this habit is established while there are just two of you, it won't be hard to maintain it when the children begin coming along.

5. Make a decision to read the Bible through each year. I've had people say this is legalism, but that's okay. Personally, I have experienced great strength and victory purely from the Word when nothing else could help. In fact, when a person calls me for marriage counseling and seems emotionally upset, (usually a woman), I tell her to sit down and in one sitting, read ten chapters and then call me back. The amazing thing has always been that when she returns my call, she is calm and able to talk reasonably. This is what God's Word does to us: it helps us see beyond our foolish thoughts and our out-of-control emotions. I know of nothing like reading the Bible that will help you refocus and enable you to have a truly *WOW* marriage. It is only by obedience to God's Word that we are able to make Jesus Lord of our lives. This also becomes another area of togetherness in the marriage, for what is better to share than the exciting principles of God's Word?

6. Never, never, never go to bed angry—*"Let not the sun go down on your wrath" (Ephesians 4:26)*— no matter what the circumstance, and always pray together before tumbling into bed. There's something really special about a husband and wife joining hands and praying together at their bedside. It is an intimate time at the close of the day, and sharing it with Jesus brings a dimension that you will always treasure. Don't allow anything to rob you of this. If one of you wants to go to bed earlier than the other then be sure to have prayer together first. My suggestion is that each of you lead in prayer, one by one, but do remember to enumerate God's blessings

of the past. Something dynamic happens in the atmosphere when we speak out our thanksgivings for God's blessings. Especially express thanksgiving for your spouse. This helps each to come before the Lord and as you melt before God, His sweetness spills over into your marriage relationship, breaking hardnesses that may be trying to form between you.

When my older sister's family was younger and her children were teenagers, I was amazed how she could have her dining table surrounded with guests, get them started on a full after-church meal, and then disappear. One spring when we were visiting in their home, I decided to walk through the house and see where she went. Since it was a school night, her children had gotten their snack immediately and had gone to bed. But when I found her, she was sitting on their beds praying with each one individually. Her guests were important, but something more important called her away—that very special pre-bedtime prayer with her teenage children, all three of whom were called into God's work. This is not only a very important part of parenting, it is also a great boost to a *WOW* marriage. Nothing can replace the power of people praying together: not only does it melt us in God's presence, it helps us to refocus and to erase the little irritations that can arise in any relationship. Paul exhorted us in 1 Timothy 2:1 to *"First of all"* make prayer a priority in our lives. If this holds in our Christian walk, how much more important it is for couples to pray together.

7. Avoid bringing anything or anyone into your home that might bring in the wrong atmosphere: this could be a book, a TV program, a person (frequently a down-and-out person you're trying to help; even a relative) or music. I've known marriages that were devastated through helping a young homeless girl who seduced the husband. The snares in this arena are

endless, and both spouses need to be on guard. Our homes must be a place of pure love and godliness in every area, and we are responsible before God to keep it that way. Remember when Boaz was making the deal to marry Ruth, and he had to deal with the nearer kinsman? The kinsman said he didn't want to mar his own inheritance by taking Ruth. And Jesus taught *"Every city or house divided against itself shall not stand."* Also, Deuteronomy 7:26 warns us not to bring any abomination into our homes. When a couple marries, their relationship must be their first priority next to God.

All other friends and relationships (even ministry) must succumb to the priority of the *WOW* marriage.

Our commitment to Jesus generates His "reigning power" in us. That's what happened on our wedding night, as, in prayer, we dedicated all that we would ever be, to Him. So, make Jesus Lord of your marriage and Lord of your future, and He will reign in every part. This is your first step and doubtless your most important one toward a truly *WOW* marriage.

Case in Point

"Can you help me?" the voice on the phone wailed. "My wife moved out a year ago, and I just don't want to live. I failed her and had an affair, but I am sorry, and will do anything to get her back. I have nothing to live for without her and our little son."

The following Tuesday they were in my office—hard, stiff, and sitting there like strangers. It was a difficult session. She talked on and on about his faults. He sat there with his eyes on the floor, saying nothing. Occasionally he whispered appealingly, "I'm sorry."

Though he took all the blame, experience has proven that there are always two sides. As he talked, the other side began to surface. I began to take notes: selfishness, personal ambition, pride, a "can't let-go-of-mama" syndrome. She and their little boy had moved in with her mother and though he had talked her into coming for counseling, she had no desire to make up.

What normally would take an hour went beyond two hours. I began to sense that this was a couple who had been religious in their past, but neither of them had a true relationship with God. The things she talked incessantly about were surface problems and the blame was all on him. Neither of them had the slightest concept of the grace of God or the power of the gospel.

It took five or six sessions (weekly) before I sensed they were ready. Though I always begin and end each counseling time with prayer, there is always that special hour when I know the Holy Spirit has prepared the heart for a new commitment. It was on a Tuesday, and both had spilled their guts in a new way, and I knew God was at work.

As soon as I could, I moved in with the simple plan of salvation, having them read Scriptures on sin and forgiveness. Both of them began to melt as I pushed the claims of Christ. We got down on our knees and I had each of them to pray aloud in their own way, asking for God's forgiveness, and then they turned to each other and asked forgiveness.

When dealing with broken couples who are asking for forgiveness, I insist that the other responds with "I forgive you." I believe this is part of the process of making Jesus Lord in every area of our lives. As we went through this little ritual, kneeling on the floor, she suddenly began to sob. He had cried many times before, but until that moment, she had remained hard, rejected, and bitter.

When she melted, something beautiful happened. Suddenly they were in each other's arms, and I felt like an intruder into a very sacred moment. The Holy Spirit was at work, and my heart was singing inside. I waited just a little and then said, "Now, not only must you make a new commitment to each other, but that commitment needs to be founded on a higher one: a commitment to the Lord Jesus Christ." They were both ready, and one by one they prayed the sinner's prayer after me, and made Jesus Lord of their lives.

"But I'm still not ready to move back in with him" she said, "as I can't ever trust him again."

I assured her that I would not push it, but that the Lord would lead them when the right time came. God would prepare her heart and give her the glow of their first love. It took several more months of weekly sessions before she was ready. They were coming to church, were both baptized, and were joyfully serving the Lord, so I had adjusted to the idea of their still being separated. It was all in God's hands. Then one day, at the beginning of the session, she spoke it out: "I moved back in last night" she said with a sparkle in her eyes that was exciting. "And our little son is so happy! But most of all, God has come into our family, and we are so thrilled!" They had discovered the joy of making Jesus Lord of their lives.

That was over fifteen years ago. Today, they and their lovely son are serving the Lord wholeheartedly. God has prospered their business, which they renamed "Vision International" and inscribed it on their business trucks. Not only are they givers to the local church, they both carry a burden for other nations and are big givers to missions. Jesus is not only Lord of their *WOW* marriage, He is also Lord of their business and finances.

2

The Unselfishness Contest

Give and it shall be given unto you; good measure,
pressed down, and shaken together, and running over,
shall men give into your bosom. For with the same
measure that ye mete . . . it shall be measured to you
again.

(Luke 6:38)

"I am so fed up with him!" the broken voice sobbed on the phone, "Every time the bills come in he leaves me. Can you help me? He's left again for the twentieth time."

"What did you do to him?" I asked. She replied that she had done nothing. But when I prodded, I found out that she had railed on him, yelled at him, and thrown hot coffee at him over money. This was the beginning of a long season of counseling.

The root of their problem was not the railing or the yelling or the coffee or the bills—it was selfishness. She was a spender, and he was a mama's boy. Every time he encountered stress, he ran home to his mother.

Shortly after our marriage, I was stunned to realize that I had married a very unselfish man, but that I was exceedingly selfish. When we had two cars, he would always take the older one and leave me the newer one, or the one with more gas. I began to realize that without a word, he gave me the preference in everything. When this dawned on me, I had a little talk with myself: "Look here, Ruth Bell, you've been a brat too long. From now on, you're going to be just as unselfish and considerate as he is. When he takes the older or worse car to work, you're going to go and leave him the better car and drive the other one home. From today on, there is going to be an 'unselfishness-contest' in this relationship."

It took some doing for me to remember this. I had been pampered ever since age five, when my younger sister died in Japan and Mother reached out to me to fill her empty arms. I had never realized how selfish I was until the day I—in shame—awakened to Johnny's unselfishness, and this filled me with remorse.

I was standing in my kitchen when this hit me like a thunder bolt. Weeping before the Lord, I asked His forgiveness and His help that I, too, might become unselfish. How I needed help to remember the contest. It was beautiful how the Lord came to my rescue. He showed me small acts to do for my beloved that I had never thought of before—little notes here and there and things to surprise him that said how much I cared.

In our affluent society, the mandate of Jesus to "*love your neighbor as yourself*" (Luke 27:10) and to "*do to others what you would have them do to you*" (Matthew 7:12) has been lost, even to most Christians. Instead, the "me-first" attitude is rampant. This me-first syndrome exchanges integrity for selfishness, and selfishness produces strife, jealousy, self pity, and anger, which prevent the marriage from fulfilling God's design of trust, love, and unselfishness. Real joy in life comes from sharing and being deliberately unselfish.

A beautiful element of Christianity is the spirit of giving. As I began to experience this daily, our marriage began to overflow with joy and excitement.

Our sex life changed. Personal feelings were not the priority. Instead, our desires were to bless and please the other. This influenced everything we did. It made marriage fun!

One day I bought a new dress that I thought was really pretty. It was modest, well-made, and I loved the style. When I showed it to Johnny, he didn't like the color. I never wore it again. He was more important to me than a dress. (I was beginning to learn to be unselfish.)

Giving to each other has become a way of life for us, and it adds lots of laughter to our marriage. If I have cash and he has spent his, it makes me eager for him to have mine. This is the fun part of the contest. And in giving and giving, the fun never stops. We both give, and in that way we are both receiving perpetually, each from the other.

If one of us wants to buy something and the other doesn't quite agree, we both make it a habit to hang loose, knowing that if God wants us to get it, we will both feel the same way. This kind of give and take has been wonderful. It comes about by honoring the other and practicing this unselfishness contest even in tiny details. It totally cancels a power struggle. It is a blend of putting the other's desires first, and underneath it all trusting God to bring us together in total agreement.

Our arguments are comedies of trying to please the other to such an extent, we sometimes do things we really didn't want to, thinking that the other person thought we wanted to, and it gets all mixed up, and really brings a lot of laughter.

This unselfishness contest is the only kind of competition that should be permitted in a good marriage. Other areas of competing with each other are off-limits and should never be entered into. Never compete for leadership; never compete in your ministries; never compete in telling interesting stories to your guests or friends. Never compete with each other in anything except in this unselfishness contest.

In sharing incidents of your life with friends or telling funny stories, avoid telling anything that would reflect unwisely on your spouse. Couples who do this often unconsciously hurt one another. Don't give indirect digs. Learn to speak things that edify and build each other up, not things that tear down. Compliment each other often.

As a girl, I loved to tell something juicy that made people oh and ah. Then my parents had me memorize Philippians 4:8:

Finally, brethren, whatsoever things are true, whatsoever things are honest, whatsoever things are just, whatsoever things are pure, whatsoever things are lovely, whatsoever things are of good report; if there be any virtue, and if there be any praise, think on these things.

Whatsoever things are lovely? Whatsoever things are of a good report? Wow! What a standard. Mother made me ask the question each time before telling some incident: Is it lovely? Is it a good report? This helped me a lot. God doesn't want us telling anecdotes at the expense of someone else, especially our spouse. I'm most grateful for God's

Word. It is like a hammer when we really need it, and has a way of hammering at us to correct us.

This verse has helped me repeatedly when I felt the impulse to tell something that would not edify and might even hurt. What does it matter if it's juicy and makes interesting conversation? If it is going to hurt someone or weaken another's influence, we should put it out of our minds and never repeat it. I believe this comes under the category of "covering for our brother or sister." Remember how God blessed Noah's two sons, Shem and Japheth, because they refused to expose their father? They went into his tent backward and covered him in his drunken stupor.

God cursed Ham, because he exposed his father. This shows two principles we need to practice in a marriage:

1. The importance of covering for the one we love.
2. The importance of honoring the delegated authority God has put over us.

These two principles are important in practicing the unselfishness contest, and they need to be used deliberately and with forethought. Ask yourself, "Is this something that might hurt my beloved?" If so, don't say it. On the other hand, don't be a wimp. If something needs to be confronted, do it gently, with humility and love, and always in private with an appeal, and choose the right timing for it. This is what Queen Esther did: she appealed to her heathen husband, chose the right timing, and God gave her a great victory.

For years, we practiced this contest of unselfishness without mentioning it. We were both semi-conscious of little incidents that made us aware of it, but it was never spoken of between us. That way, there was never a sense of disappointment or accusation if one of us forgot.

When you continually set your will to compete with your spouse to be more unselfish, this generates in you a desire to give and give and give some more. Luke 6:38 says our giving will produce an overflow of giving back to us, pressed down, shaken together, and running over. This cannot fail, as it is a major promise in the Bible.

It not only works when we give to God's kingdom, it works wonderfully in a marriage. One of the biggest hindrances, and most common causes of marital breakups, is selfishness. Selfishness produces a power struggle, creates arguments over money, and takes you into debt and an obsession for things you don't need. Throw away the credit cards. Refuse to get any new ones.

Selfishness is also at the root of many problems based on jealousy which the Bible warns against. It is cruel as the grave. Many couples go through life miserable because they have not dealt with this weakness. I know of couples who are so jealous of each other, they stay angry most of the time. If they go out to eat, and he happens to look at a pretty lady, their evening is ruined. Or, if she comes home from work thirty minutes later than usual, it makes for a big fight. She can't go to the store without his being jealous.

One day, early in our marriage, I told myself, "Ruth Bell, you will never allow yourself to be jealous, ever." I made a quality decision to completely trust my husband. As a minister, there would be circumstances that could create a problem between us if I allowed jealousy to control me.

This decision not to be jealous set me free, and helped build trust between us. It is the same principle as making the decision to submit, or deciding to forgive. The decision helps you control your feelings when they want to go out of bounds. When you tie this to the unselfishness contest, it helps prevent you from a silly pity party.

Only God has the right to be jealous. That is because He must be number one in our hearts, and no one else is to replace Him, ever. When a couple is competing in the unselfishness contest, there is no room for jealousy. The first priority is to please the other, and not one's self. When a person knows his spouse's first desire is to please him, jealousy finds no place. As trust increases, jealousy is cancelled. The giving spirit brings into the marriage many good things: honor, respect, mutual submission, concern, sensitivity, understanding, patience and space. Some of these will be discussed later, but the unselfishness contest is a major key, and is the second step in your *WOW* marriage. Decide now to have an ongoing contest between you to see which one can be the most unselfish.

Case in Point

Jeff and Jennifer were a beautiful couple with four little girls. They had been saved for nearly a year, when Jennifer dropped out of church. When we asked about her, Jeff hung his head in embarrassment. Finally one day he told us she had moved out and was having an affair with another man. Jeff continued to come to church and remained true. Our hearts wrapped around him and his daughters. He was rejected and hurt, wondering if the agony would ever end. Just as he was beginning to let go, she called to say she was pregnant and that the sonogram showed it was a boy, and since her boyfriend had now run off, could she come back to him, and would he receive the baby as his own?

Jeff was bewildered and wounded more than ever. What should he do? He had always wanted a son, but not someone else's! And could he ever trust Jennifer again? She had wandered far, far away from God. Would she be a bad influence on their little girls now? He asked if he could bring her for counseling.

I expected the first counseling session to be difficult. Jennifer had been away from the Lord now several years and I thought she would be hard and resentful. But no, she was broken and repentant. She not only begged Jeff for forgiveness for her immorality, but for her selfishness and the deception she had lived with. In one sentence after another, she began to pour out her remorse, telling us how God had dealt with her for her selfishness and pride. That her selfishness was at the root of her immorality and she wanted no more of it. She begged for forgiveness for the weaknesses in her character, and spoke about how unselfish Jeff was. She told how she lay in bed at night in the arms of the other man, thinking about Jeff who had always put her and the girls first, who never thought about himself, but gave and served. She would tell herself what a fool she was to give up Jeff, the man of integrity, for the other man who took and took from her, then left her high and dry when she became pregnant.

"Can you ever forgive me?" she sobbed. "If you'll give me another chance, I believe God will replace my selfishness with unselfishness and we can make it a contest between us." (I had taught them about the unselfishness contest in an adult Sunday School class.)

There were many more counseling times after that, in order for them to be welded back together as a family. It was extremely difficult for Jeff at first. Could he truly love her again? Could he genuinely forgive? Could he ever love the baby boy as his own?

As we met together week after week, I laid the principles of this book heavily upon them. I especially stressed the importance of the lordship of Jesus in their lives, and the unselfishness contest. She picked it right up, and initiated all kinds of cute ways to beat him at the game of unselfishness. Gradually, our sessions together became less water-soaked (no more tears) and filled with laughter.

Today they are joyfully serving the Lord. However, one thing has become a "thing" with the whole family— even the four little girls are aware of its power—and that's the importance of the "unselfishness contest."

3

Joyfully Serving Each Other

By love, serve one another.

(Galatians 5:13)

Our society loves to be served. More and more, families go out to eat, rather than to cook and serve one another.

An affluent society enjoys being served by others. If we're not careful, this spirit of wanting to be served rather than to serve gets into our marriages and family relationships.

My older sister, Faith, is an expert in serving others. When we visit in her home, it overflows with good food, lots of guests, and warm hospitality. Many times I've sat at her table, trying to think of what might be needed so I could help her serve. But she is always faster than I to see the needs of others such as a fill-up on tea or coffee.

I think this began when she was a child. While I was being pampered and spoiled, she was Mother's right arm. She was four years older than I, and even when we were very young, I remember how she helped sweep the porches and walks, iron the clothes, and take care of us kids, always joyfully helping Mother, or quickly seeing the needs at the table and serving everyone.

Jesus, teaching about greatness in Matthew 20:26-28, said: "*Whosoever will be great among you, let him be your minister* [servant]; *and whosoever will be chief among you, let him be your servant* [slave]. *Even as the Son of man came not to be ministered unto, but to minister, and to give his life.*"

The whole world will stand aside and make room for any individual who will be willing to be a true servant. The way to success is to serve others. This is so in the business world, and it is also true in a *WOW* marriage. Whenever a spirit of serving and humility reigns, it brings with it beautiful harmony.

When we desire to serve one another, rather than be served, it takes away all thought of comparing our workload or wanting the other to do more. Rather, it gives us fulfillment in what we do for each other. Serving based on love is endless.

I've had to address this problem frequently in marriage counseling. It is especially prominent in marriages where both husband and wife work. In this kind of relationship, the principle of joyfully serving one another becomes very important, but it can also be difficult.

One thing that helps develop a serving attitude is to give all our expectations to God. As a young pastor's wife,

I discovered this principle and its importance in my relationship with wives of guest ministers. I heard older pastors' wives complain about guests in their home who never helped with the cooking and housework. This helped me make a quality decision.

I decided to give my expectations to God and to always tell my guests: "I want you to relax while you're here. I don't expect you to help with the cooking, or dishes, or anything." I found that this decision not only freed the visiting lady, but it did something wonderful in me. It cancelled out ahead of time resentment I might have felt had I been expecting help from my guests and they failed to deliver. It was like redeeming the situation before it happened. As it was, because I didn't expect it, whenever they did insist on helping, it was a pleasant surprise.

Bill Gothard in his "Institute in Basic Life Conflicts" has a beautiful teaching on "Giving all your expectations back to God." Every young married couple would be greatly blessed by attending one of his seminars. He teaches heavily on Bible principles that help us to flow together in unselfishness, making Jesus Lord.

Newlyweds often come into the new relationship with many preconceived ideas about each other, and when these ideas don't materialize, they are disappointed. This isn't right. We should not expect our spouse to be like our mom or sister, or some other elegant person. We must accept the mate God gave us. Leave any changing that needs to be done, up to the Lord, for He is expert in making changes in our lives and character (though He does seem to take His time doing it).

Think in terms of what you do for your spouse or your children, as actually doing it unto the Lord Jesus. The Lord said, "*Whatsoever you do to the least of these, you do it unto me.*"

25

If Jesus were in your home and needed His laundry done, wouldn't you do it joyfully? If He were hungry, wouldn't you delight in cooking Him a lovely meal? When you serve your mate, or clean up a mess after him, or pick up his clothes, say in your heart, "Thank You, Lord, for the privilege of serving my husband and You."

Instead of grumbling at each other, or criticizing, it is much more *WOW* to serve one another joyfully. I'm not saying we should never help one another to improve. There were times in our early marriage when I rolled my husband's socks into a ball, laughingly hollered, "Catch it!" and threw them at him as he was shaving. This was not done in anger, but in fun. Sometimes they landed in the commode. It was done in play as an act of camaraderie. Humor is also an important part of our *WOW* marriage.

You don't have to be a wimp to be a joyful servant. Serving is something we learn by discipline and by doing. It is deliberate, and helps to make a marriage fun. But it must be done joyfully. Psalms 100:2 says *"Serve the Lord with gladness"* and that is how God wants us to serve one another.

In Deuteronomy 28:41 and 47, God said our children would go into captivity unless we serve Him with joyfulness and gladness. Many parents are faithful to teach their children the "do's" and "don'ts" of life. In fact, sometimes the don'ts outweigh the do's. But where is the joy and gladness?

When mothers and fathers have taught their children God's ways and they've gone astray, it makes the parents wonder where they failed. In many cases it was because God's guidelines were taught without the principle of His joy. The above Scripture teaches the importance of a balance between God's laws and serving with gladness and joy. I've known pastors' children who left their faith because they said there was no joy in their home, only criticism. This is tragic.

The roots of this tragedy can begin early in the marriage. Often it begins with comparing our workloads, or one member of the relationship having a "pity party," which God abhors. A pity party is a release for the moment, but it does not bring glory to God. It also does dreadful damage to our emotions and our marriage. So how do we handle resentment when we feel we are being used or abused? We redeem it ahead of time. We have a little discussion with ourselves. We say, "Now look here. You will not feel sorry for yourself when you come home from work tired, and you have to cook, and he is sitting on the couch relaxing." If this fails, laugh it away and be joyful about it, without any resentment. It's a decision you make.

I first heard this concept of redeeming a situation before it happens by the setting of my will in a family life seminar some years ago. In the same way that I made a quality decision to never be jealous, I made the decision to serve my husband with joy. Did you know you don't have to give in to jealousy or laziness?

When I knew I was marrying a minister, I made a quality decision to never be jealous and to try to be a joyful servant. I knew there would be times when women would think they were in love with my husband. And there have been a few. A pastor who is loved by his people is vulnerable to all sorts of situations. When he leads someone to Jesus, it is easy for them to innocently mistake that fresh godly love for romantic love. It is important for a pastor's wife that she not entertain a spirit of mistrust or jealousy. We should not be careless or naive in this area. [This subject is dealt with more fully in Chapter 11.] We must always be accountable to each other. If a real problem arises, then, without jealousy or being uptight, there needs to be an understanding between you and your mate so that perfect trust can be built and maintained.

Another side to this needs to be addressed here. God gave us two sons who were a source of great joy to us. However, I went through a period of resenting the way they left our bathroom: towels in all directions, mirrors all splattered up, soap swimming in water, bath and shower quite messy. Sound familiar?

Most of us like a neat house, and I've always felt that if the beds were made, the kitchen clean, and the bathrooms tidy, I wouldn't feel embarrassed if unexpected company came. Try as hard as I might, the bathrooms stayed messy no matter how many times a day I worked on them. I secretly resented this for years, without redeeming the situation ahead as I learned later in the seminar.

Finally, tired of feeling resentful, I chose a good time and bared my heart to the family. Wouldn't you know it? They were sweet about it, and apologized and promised to help me keep it neat and clean. And they did. I thought later, how foolish I was to keep that resentment in my heart all those years, when, with just a little appeal, they were willing to cooperate. This is why, sometimes, a gentle confrontation is wiser than trying to stifle something that bothers you.

How do we serve God joyfully? It begins with the new couple serving one another. And how do we serve one another? By doing everything we can to lighten the load of our spouse; by delighting when he relaxes on the couch and we cannot. Life has a way of balancing things out.

So, without hesitation, or reservation, let's move out into a joyful servanthood toward our spouse—serving him or her just as we would the Lord Jesus.

For years, one of our sons gave me fits over his messy room. I fussed about it, nagged him, bribed him, and tried several ways to get him to hang up his clothes, all to no avail. Finally I turned to prayer.

When I asked the Lord how to handle it, He spoke right back to me: "Serve him by doing it for him, and get him used to the tidy environment." Not only did this help him, for later he became very tidy, it did something good in me. It set me free from resentment and he expressed an appreciation for me that was not there before.

This then is our third step in having a *WOW* marriage. Begin today to think up ways in which you can take delight in serving your spouse—and your family—with joy.

Case in Point

"I don't even like him" said Lisa with tears. "This is my second marriage and I'm through."

Lisa had been seriously ill and had acquired the habit of laying around all day, doing nothing. When David came home from work, he found her in bed, the house a mess, no supper being prepared and their two small children running wild.

"He bores me. I don't want to see him, and I just want out" she said over and over. Here was a young woman that only three months before had nearly died. Now she had been dismissed by her doctor as cured and could go back to work. But she had no goals, no interests and no desires. Even my appeal to her on the basis of her children's needs made no dent. She was thinking only of herself and her boredom with life.

David claimed to be an atheist, but otherwise, he was a good husband. He put up with a lot without grumbling about her. She was a church member and had a lot of friends, but one by one they were drained by her incessant requests for help, and their friendship became strained.

Where do you start in a counseling situation like this? There was no drinking problem, no unfaithfulness morally as far as I could detect, but she kept insisting she wanted out. Telling her how God hates divorce made no impact. Warning her about the difficulties of a single mother trying to raise her children alone made no difference.

As always, I prayed for the direction of the Holy Spirit. Almost immediately that still small voice whispered into my spirit, "Challenge her with a life of joyfully serving her husband and children. Paint a vivid picture for her. Help her see how different life could be if she got up and bathed and fixed her hair and made herself and her home beautiful with fun and sunshine. Have cookies in the oven filling the house with a welcoming fragrance when the kids return from school. Have a gorgeous dinner ready when David comes home from work. Play Christian music and hum God's praises throughout the day as she serves her family with joy."

So I jumped in with principle number three: "Joyfully Serving Each Other." At first she gave me a "horse" laugh. But the more she pushed her argument of how impossible that would be, the more the Holy Spirit nudged me to press this truth further. Finally I had to say, "Unless you take the first step toward this principle of becoming 'a new you,' I can't see you again. When I said that, her whole attitude changed."

"Do you really think I can change?" she asked with a flicker of hope in her dead-looking eyes.

"I know you can," I answered. "And I'll help you walk through it. All I ask is that you do what I suggest, and try real hard. God will give the strength and wisdom, and will make up for whatever else is lacking."

So we began. When I challenged her with a lovely hot meal for her husband when he comes home from work, she threw all sorts of excuses at me. "He clutters the table with all his business papers and brings his work home with him, and I don't dare touch anything. So where would we eat?"

I told her to stack everything in a corner of the room, then put it all back after she had (immediately) cleaned off the table.

Again she made a face at me. It was a faith walk all the way through. But each week when she came for her appointment, I saw exciting improvements. Her attitude was beginning to change. She was smiling more and there was a whole new beauty about her that expressed itself in the twinkle in her eyes.

One day David called me. "What have you been doing to my wife?" he asked. "Hey! I like it! Not only is she a fabulous cook, our home is full of joy and laughter for the first time in years. I can't begin to thank you enough! And we are falling in love all over again!"

This principle of serving the other with joy has a deeper root, and I began to see that the deeper root had to be confronted also. Lisa wasn't lazy, for she had held an excellent job before her illness. Lisa's problem was a combination of principles 1, 2, and 3: she had never really made Jesus Lord of her marriage; nor had she ever treated David as her head; and the unselfishness contest was totally foreign to both of them. When she began working on principle number 3, and really putting her heart into joyfully serving her family, the Holy Spirit began to deal with her in other areas. The progression was beautiful to watch. A few weeks later, David began to come to church with her. And the night he went to the altar, a true miracle unfolded before our eyes.

Today this couple is happily serving the Lord together and teaching their children God's wonderful principles of serving others with joy.

4

Refuse Strife and Criticism

Foolish and unlearned questions avoid, knowing that they do gender strifes. And the servant of the Lord must not strive; but be gentle.

(2 Timothy 2:23, 24a)

Cutdowns and criticism are among the greatest hindrances to a *WOW* marriage. Every married person would be wise to determine to give his spouse at least seven compliments a day. I give this advice to everyone.

We do this in our marriage. Sometimes we count them laughingly on our fingers. Though we know that we are doing it deliberately, compliments and appreciation work miracles and are fun.

A lady with grown children had to start baby-sitting her grandson. "Lord, please help me," she prayed. "When my children were little I used to get irritated and yell at them, and I don't want to be that way again. Can you help me Lord to keep calm regardless?" She prayed a specific prayer, asking for extra patience and made a quality decision to never let herself get uptight or impatient with her grandson.

Years later her testimony was that, to her surprise, through all that season she never once lifted her voice or became irritated. She was amazed that she could remain calm and sweet no matter how difficult the situations were. Just a quality decision along with prayer had made a tremendous difference. She said later she wished some older person had told her about these keys to harmony when her own children were young.

This same type of decision works wonderfully in a marriage. Though none of us is perfect, and neither of us is the ideal mate, when we constantly ravish the other with words of appreciation and affection, it projects acceptance and creates trust and security. A marriage without trust is a flimsy relationship.

Frequently people ask "How can you think of seven compliments a day?" It's easy, once you make it a lifestyle. When my husband asks me if his tie looks okay, I answer "Honey, you couldn't look tacky if you tried." And that's true. The compliments we give each other (even laughingly) are genuine. This adds fun to the marriage, and brings a positive atmosphere into the home.

There are a million ways we can compliment each other. Here are a few:

1. You do such a great job with the lawn. You even look great in your old, sweaty work clothes.

2. It's wonderful just to be near you.
3. Thank you for being such a great daddy and grandpa to our kids.
4. What an honor it is to be your wife.
5. I love your embraces.
6. It's a joy, not a task, to do your laundry.
7. It's wonderful to have you home.
8. You are my very best friend. I can tell you anything.
9. No one touches my heart like you do.
10. I'd rather hear you pray than anyone.
11. Thanks for taking out the garbage.
12. Thanks for a lovely meal.

Never allow yourselves to call each other derogatory names or threaten divorce or separation. This is a total "no-no." Have there been irritations in our *WOW* marriage? Sure. There have been many. Resentments? A few. But thank God, the word divorce and "splitting up" has not been spoken even once—never—in over fifty years of marriage.

Someone asked me how we handle our tiffs and disagreements. They couldn't believe that two such different people could live together so long without at least one of them feeling angry enough to at least threaten to leave. The person asked: "What happens to your *WOW* marriage when one of you is angry?" Our reply was: "We are in covenant forever and a little tiff or anger has nothing to do with changing our *WOW* marriage. It is for keeps—like a solid foundation under us that cannot be changed. A true covenant is never affected by anger, hurts, or disappointments. If it is a covenant, feelings or circumstances have nothing to do with it. It is forever!"

This is what marriage is: a permanent covenant forever. The Bible says that as sparks fly upward, man's days are full of troubles. When problems arise (and they do), we both muster every effort to untangle the situation at once. The Bible says to not let the sun go down on our wrath. Don't allow any time to build up a misunderstanding with false imaginations, mulling over and over what was said. Be quick to take the blame and apologize.

Many divorces develop through strife, and most of them are avoidable. This is sad, as it causes a dreadful fracturing of the child's emotions. Most divorced children think they are to blame—maybe because they did not feed the dog or take out the garbage when told to. Galatians 5:15 says: *"But if ye bite and devour one another, take heed that ye be not consumed one of another."*

Don't pick at each other over petty annoyances. Some couples argue over which end of the toothpaste should be squeezed first—the top or the bottom; or how the toilet paper should be on the roll, or over such petty things as closing the cupboard doors in the kitchen.

Before you criticize your spouse, ask yourself how important the issue is. Ask if that comment is going to help or hurt your relationship. Ask yourself if the issue at stake is more important than your *WOW* marriage, or your spouse's probable reaction to your words.

Many of the issues we fret over don't materialize, and all that worrying is for nothing. The same goes for little nitpicking things that couples say to each other. The Bible warns that if we do this, we are biting and devouring each other, and this will consume us.

One morning as my husband left our school chapel, a student stopped him to remark about a white spot on his dark coat sleeve. Evidently he had brushed against something white and it stood out. His answer to the student was, "Yes, but look at my other sleeve, and the back and front of the coat, isn't it lovely and clean?" The student got the point. If we are not careful, that's how we treat our partners in marriage—always picking at little flaws and overlooking all the good parts that are there. Let's begin to focus on their good points by giving seven compliments each day.

Some people quarrel over decisions about their children. There should be no power struggle here. It is not worth the division it can bring. When done before the children it is exceedingly harmful. Pitting one parent against the other, not only confuses the children, it sows seeds of disrespect and rebellion into their lives.

Strife inflicts deep wounds, words are spoken that are not easily forgotten bringing confusion to the relationship. Children who are subjected to strife become disoriented and insecure. And as they grow older, they fall into the same cycle of strife, and eventually take it with them into their own marriages. The scenario is repeated in their own family.

When parents disagree about a decision affecting a child, the discussion should always be done in private. Children should only see their parents in total agreement. Frequently, the mother will have information that the dad needs. Rather than giving opportunity for the child to think they are divided, it is wise to give this information privately, and then, if it changes the decision, announce together that the former answer is now reversed.

Usually the issue at stake is not as important as the need for the family to be in unity. Strife is something that you can make a quality decision to resist. When strife is caused by a power struggle, it is good to remember that two heads make a monster. Sometimes this springs from rebellion, or a lack of willingness to submit to authority: either God's authority or the husband's. This is an important area in all of us. If we first make a quality commitment to be submitted to God, and secondly are determined to be submitted to our mate, it will dispel all motivation for strife and criticism. It takes two to quarrel, and if one of you refuses to enter into strife it simply can't develop. James

3:16 says: *"Where envying and strife is, there is confusion and every evil work."*

I heard a lady tell about going to church one morning with her hair totally out of control. She said it looked terrible, even after she washed it three times. At church, her best friend came up to her and laughed with her about her hair. It didn't bother her as this was her best friend, and she had decided to not let it affect her.

But in a few minutes another lady, of whom she wasn't very fond, came up and laughed about her hair, and actually said the very same words. Suddenly she felt anger rising up. As she thought about it, she realized her irritation was based on her decision. With one she had decided not to get angry, and with the other she decided to let resentment arise, which led to strife.

Giving lots of compliments daily to the one you love helps you to purposely avoid criticisms and cutdowns. God has not called us to be our partner's conscience or to remake our spouse, but He has called us to be encouragers and peacemakers. At least four times in Scripture we are told to "seek peace" (Psalm 34:14; Jeremiah 29:7; Hebrews 12:14; 1 Peter 3:11).

When we refuse strife and criticism and instead, joyfully lavish upon our mate as many compliments as we can it lights up his day. It brings confidence, trust and appreciation into the relationship. Appreciation really does beget appreciation. In order to do this, there will be times when we must bridle our tongue. James 1:26 says: *"If any man among you seem to be religious, and bridleth not his tongue, but deceiveth his own heart, this man's religion is vain."*

Have you ever walked in a mall, determined to make everyone you meet smile? It's like giving compliments. Through a simple smile, you are saying to the people you meet: "I accept you. I appreciate your humanness, for you were made in God's image."

I learned from a friend, to say "Bless you" to clerks who wait on me. That's a phrase everyone appreciates. It has a tremendous meaning. It specifically means "I empower you to prosper." Most people haven't a clue as to its meaning, and sometimes I'll ask, "Do you know what that means?" Often, they'll say they do, but when asked further, they hesitate, and then admit they really don't know. But when the meaning is given, they always respond with a warm "Thank you!"

With the effect such simple words as "thank you" and "bless you" have upon a total stranger, think what compliments and appreciation do in a marriage.

There are seven elements of loving support that, when entered into deliberately, will help you to avoid strife:

1. **Unconditional Commitment** - You both make an unconditional commitment to avoid strife, and to build each other up at all times: with seven compliments a day.

2. **Scheduled Time Together** - Together plan fun times. Don't allow your lives to be so busy and serious you can't relax together and enjoy each other. We try to swim together at least once a week. We play Scrabble together, planning times to simply relax and just be us (away from the telephone).

3. **Be Available for Your Spouse** - Don't permit outside responsibilities to crowd out your good times together. Go on a date, just the two of you.

4. **Tender Treatment** - Always exert the utmost tenderness toward each other, even as you did while you were dating. Stand together always. Be loyal.

5. **Eye Contact** - Remember how you looked deeply into each other's eyes while you were courting? Do that often now. Loving eye contact helps to erase hurts and irritations. Let your eyes overflow with love and admiration.

6. Listening With Understanding - Really listen! And try to wear the shoes of the other, and understand where he is coming from, and how he feels. Express your understanding with compassion. When we enter into that which he is sharing with us, it says how much we care, and enhances his importance. (Even when we think we have a better idea.)

7. Touching: On our honeymoon, we couldn't stand to sit across the table from each other at our meals. We wanted to feel each other every minute. This is something we need to practice and continue in the marriage—the warmth of each other's flesh; holding each other when we meet in the hallway. Hug each other often. Cuddle with or without sex. Focus on the importance of the closeness of our love. Keep it up. An embrace often gives new hope and strength to the other. Once, when our son David was having severe pains in his heart, my husband stood and just held him tight. Years later, he still told people how that gave him strength and dispelled his fears.

These are simple yet powerful ways to help you avoid strife. However, the quickest and easiest way to learn on a daily basis, is to give seven compliments a day. Remember, we are created in God's image, and should constantly reinforce the godly characteristics in one another. Compliment these attributes often—things grow when the sun shines. And since God delights in our praises, how much more we as humans take new courage, and relationships are enhanced, by the praises of those we love. So begin now to give your spouse at least seven compliments a day, and always refuse strife and that which may cause it. This is step number four in having a *WOW* marriage.

Case in Point

"I'm going to shoot my brains out" Laura said as she burst into my office at 8 o'clock one morning. "Why would you do that?" I asked as I led her to a chair and tried to calm my loudly pounding heart.

"George and I fight all the time and I'm tired of it. He drinks and he gambles and now I'm sure he's seeing another woman. I've asked him to come with me for counseling, but he refuses. There's no hope for us, so I want to end it all."

When I asked where she attended church, she looked dazed. She had been fasting, and was bitter at God because her marriage seemed to get more unbearable by the hour. I began to sense that the whole problem was one of strife and constant criticism. She criticized George because he never went to church, never read his Bible, never prayed, and wasn't teaching their three children anything about God. He was a good provider and was never violent, but they argued constantly and he was always criticizing her.

"Put-downs, cut-downs, and criticism," the Holy Spirit seemed to say to me. And I knew at the roots of strife were pride, selfishness, and lack of trust in God's sovereignty. How was I to help Laura through this crisis? As I prayed, I was reminded of a Scripture that I had used many times before when people were at their wits' end. I opened her Bible to Jeremiah 30:17:

I will restore health unto thee, and I will heal thee of thy wounds, saith the Lord; because they called thee an outcast, saying, This is Zion whom no man seeketh after.

She stared at me with a startled look in her eyes—like she had just seen a truth that was new to her—a bright light had just been turned on in her soul—hope was being born.

Knowing how powerful the Word is, I began laying one Scripture after another on her concerning strife and criticism and how God abhors both. I told her that in God's sight fasting and being religious is not near as important as her living the life that He has given her. That her responsibility toward God was that she fulfill His destiny for the gift of life that He had given her, and to raise her three children to become a godly seed for the nation. Her children needed to see her strong, so they could become strong. She must begin trusting God with her life and their future, knowing that He would be faithful to see her through.

I told her that more than the condemnation over killing herself, she should feel the heart of God's disappointment in her not trusting Him through her struggles. By giving up she was saying that God had failed her, and He could not help her through these difficulties. I drew some little sketches there for her, showing how things can change in our lives when we surrender fully to God's plan and destiny, and stop reacting to our feelings when things happen that we don't like. I challenged her to begin treating George the same way she would treat Jesus Christ if He entered her home and to bite her tongue when tempted to say something negative.

I showed her that more important than any ministry she could have, was her ministry to her children. No one could impact them to the degree that she could—they needed to know of a surety that nothing could ever detract her from her walk with the Lord. Her responsibility was not only godly motherhood, but also to stand against strife and criticism. Her criticizing the children's father would do more to harm them than anything he could ever do by his poor example. A major task in training her children was showing them a life of peace through Christ—a life totally void of criticism and negatives. She needed to be a Christian who would refuse to cop out or succumb to circumstances, but with God's grace would rise up and walk through the difficulties with His joy.

Her walls of resistance to God's Word seemed to begin crumbling. So I zapped her with the big gun: "The real reason you wanted to end your life" I said, "was your rebellion against God."

I drew her the sketch of God at the top, the umbrella, (husband) and the woman under it, showing her need to surrender her whole life into God's hands and to trust Him to change George in His own way and His own time. But now she had some important things to do, and I listed them on a small sheet of paper:

1. Repent for wanting to end your life.
2. Know your place as a godly wife and mother.
3. Refuse to be moved by emotions.
4. Determine to only always be moved by biblical principles instead.
5. Get into a good Bible teaching church and attend regularly.
6. Get under the care of a godly pastor.
7. Begin to treat George just as you would the Lord Jesus.

Next I gave her an assignment to write out the details of each of the above points as she performed them, and to bring them to me the following week. We got on our knees and I led her in a prayer of repentance. I helped her memorize Philippians 4:8, the Scripture that blessed me as a child, especially that part that says: "*. . . whatsoever things are just, whatsoever things are pure, whatsoever things are lovely, whatsoever things are of good report . . . think on these things.*" We said it over and over and over, until she could say it back to me without reading it.

I gave her paper and pencil and had her write down all the good things she could think of about her husband, at least 25. We made an appointment for the following week and she left after thanking me profusely and hugging me over and over. Her eyes sparkled with tears of joy, and again I thanked God for the power in His written Word.

But that's not the end of the story. After about five sessions with Laura, I received a call from her husband George. "What have you done to my wife?" He asked. "Whatever you're doing, it's like a miracle. I thought our marriage was over. We were fighting all the time. But now things are changing. Could I come with her to the next counseling appointment?"

The following week they came together, and because Laura had made such a strong point of how opposed George was to anything spiritual, after a word of prayer together, I said to him, "George, this book (holding up my Bible) has the answer for every problem, and it is only by it that I counsel. I don't have time to waste, and I don't want to waste your time. I'm not interested in your becoming 'religious' but before we start, I must have your commitment that you will do whatever the Bible says concerning whatever issue we talk about. Otherwise, it is wise to end this session right here."

To my surprise, George agreed! And as we went through several Scriptures together, I sensed he was ready to receive Jesus as Savior. At the end of the hour, we all got down on our knees and I asked him if he would like to be saved. Right there in my office, he turned his life over to the Lord with tears in his eyes. It was wonderful. They put their children in a Christian school and today are attending a fine Bible-teaching church. God gets all the glory.

5

Never Compare

And they measuring themselves by themselves, and
comparing themselves among themselves are not wise.
(2 Corinthians 10:12)

No relationship can long endure when constant comparisons are made. God says this is not wise. We should not compare our husbands with other men, our children with others, or our houses, our cars, or salaries.

We once knew two ministers who worked closely together. It was a beautiful God-given relationship, and as long as they flowed in harmony, God blessed them. Then one couple began this comparing thing and it was awful. They said to the other couple: "We do all the work and you get all the gravy." That relationship soon broke down completely and it was a reproach to God's kingdom.

When we compare people it devaluates them. It says "I don't accept you as you are. I wish you were like someone else." Instead of a compliment, it is a cutdown, and must be avoided.

The ministry brings many temptations to compare one's mate with others. Whether in preaching, teaching, music or worship, it becomes a snare. Paul taught that this is not wise. Why? God has given to each of us a special personality, a special anointing, and a special calling. When we try to copy another's ministry we are not fulfilling God's plan.

In the fifties and sixties we did church planting in Japan, and there we learned that one of the biggest hindrances to missionary work is this sin of comparing. On the mission field there are greater hazards in this area: hazards of comparing the ability to speak the language or the ability to draw and train capable, spiritual nationals.

Another big hazard in this area not common in one's own native country is the financial support; especially where several couples come from the same area and know the same Christian friends and supporters. One family may receive more backing than the other and this can pose a problem.

Comparing leads to competition, and this often leads to strife and jealousy in ministry. God wants us to be servants and givers, helping each other in ministry, not competing.

I knew a man once who said he listened to tapes of famous preachers, memorized their sermons—sentences and words—and looked in the mirror and practiced their mannerisms. Today, he is no longer in the ministry. He never found God's particular anointing for himself. He never found God's plan. He constantly compared himself with others.

Early in our ministry, I asked my husband why he didn't preach like Billy Graham. Isn't that awful? I am ashamed of it now. In those days I compared him frequently—his sermons, his delivery and his following or lack of it. Yet he stayed sweet and humble about it. One day God showed me 2 Corinthians 10:12 and I was convicted of my wrong. I did a lot of apologizing. God showed me Johnny's uniqueness, that He was using him to meet needs that others could not fill, that he was a special person, and how wrong I was to compare him to others. I'm grateful for that lesson for now I know that no matter how gifted, famous, or ordinary, each person has a vital place in God's plan.

We make comparisons between people because we do not fully understand their unique value. Created in the likeness of God, each of us is a package of dynamic potential. In my youth I was not aware of the importance of this diversity.

But the years have changed that. We now see unlimited potential, not only in my husband, but in our sons and the people to whom we minister. The human person is a miracle, filled with explosive possibilities. The first time the Lord gave Johnny a new song I laughed at it. It was all Scripture and was beautiful, but when he sang it to me, I disdained it. I had an attitude of false humility that anything birthed by either of us, would be second class. When he sang it to some college students they raved over it and began to sing it everywhere, and I had to change my mind. It was called "Line Upon Line" and has spread to many churches in America. In fact, one ministry couple made a record with it.

Any time we fall into the trap of comparing, we become blinded to the value of the other person. As parents our decisions should never be based on what other families do or don't do, but rather on what God desires for our family.

Children frequently ask for permission for something questionable on the basis that their friends get to do it, or even worse, "everybody's doing it"—which should never influence our decision. Sometimes married couples hear about sexual perversions that other couples experiment with, (usually to the demeaning of the wife). Later they wonder what went wrong. Some sexual perversions came from the homosexual community. In such an intimate area, married couples should avoid comparing with others. Whether it is in the sexual realm or elsewhere, anything that demeans one member of the relationship is harmful and can destroy a good marriage. If we are true to our commitment to have an ongoing unselfishness contest, we will give no consideration to anything that demeans the other.

I counseled a young woman once whose husband could only be turned on sexually by tying her up and beating her with his metal belt buckle. She showed me her wounds and bruises. This was selfishness in the first degree. No woman should stay in a situation like that. Yet thousands of marriages are plagued with this kind of cruelty.

I frequently have women tearfully ask if they must have oral sex when their husband demands it. This is perversion. Some Christian leaders say anything in a marriage is permissible as long as both parties agree to it. I have yet to talk with a woman who enjoys performing this act. It is demeaning to her womanhood, and will turn her against the relationship eventually.

My advice is, stay way from anything that comes from the homosexual community, and/or is demeaning to either partner. The wife is to be made the queen of the home. This must carry through in all areas of daily life, and it doesn't come through comparing her to others. Man, if you make her your queen, she will be eager to make you her king.

Christianity has always put womanhood on a high plane, and a man who honors his wife's desires is a man who himself will be honored and respected. But a demanding attitude, whether in the bedroom or the kitchen, will only bring sorrow to the marriage. God has a much higher standard, and when we follow His principles, these evil traps are avoided.

"Could I have a few words with you" asked a minister whom we had never seen before. We had just had a pastors' fellowship luncheon at a restaurant. The three of us slipped into a booth to talk.

"I felt bitterness toward you from the moment I saw you" he said, "and want to get this out of my system." When we asked if we had done anything to cause this, he said no, but that he hated some relatives of ours because he felt he had been mistreated by them. "In fact," he said, reaching down for his briefcase, "I have a manuscript here for a book I plan to publish, exposing these people."

This man was overflowing with bitterness and unforgiveness, and somehow had let the spirit of comparing transfer his hatred to us, whom he had never seen before. All we could do was appeal to him to burn the manuscript and forgive, and let God deal with the situation. We told him that God's Word commands us to give only a good report, and holding on to bitterness would eventually make him sick.

Apparently he did forgive as, after prayer together, the situation seemed to dissolve. Since then, when we meet him, there seems to be no more strain. God has taken care of it. But that hatred and bitterness was the result of comparing. This is a very dangerous tool that Satan uses to bring division. Don't let him use it in any relationship or in your marriage.

Racism is the result of the spirit of comparing. Hatred for people of certain races is often because a person has been pre-prejudiced by some hurtful experience, and this spirit of comparing produces a fear that everyone of that race will be the same. This is not the case. Whatever the race, each individual is made in the image of God, is distinctly different one from the other, and of great worth.

The key here is to remember your uniqueness in God, and never allow yourself to compare your spouse, or anyone, with others or their behavior. You and your mate are both made in God's image. You are unique. The most important part of your relationship is that both of you please the Lord in all things at all times. Treasure that uniqueness, and let God develop His fullness in you both through His ongoing creative work in you.

Your mate is unique. Your marriage is unique. Let God make your home uniquely blessed. Know that you both are different—you both are special. And as the children come, each one is unique and different. Delight in this uniqueness. Never, never compare! This is principle number five in developing a *WOW* marriage.

Decide now that you will not compare your spouse with others. You will never compare your children, or your in-laws, or anyone or anything, but will begin to delight in the uniqueness of each and every one of God's creations.

Case in Point

Bob and Mary were a beautiful couple. They were both tall and stately, well-dressed—one would think they had all the good things in life. But hours of counseling seemed to bring them no peace. It was the second marriage for both and at different times, they had each attempted suicide.

Bob it seemed was a procrastinating dreamer. He was always going to land that terrific job that would get them out of their financial struggles, but seldom kept a job for very long.

Mary was possessed with resentment as she compared herself constantly to Bob's first wife who lived two short blocks from them. For some reason Bob felt compelled to go by the house of his first wife on his way home from work each day and make sure she wasn't in need. It never seemed to occur to him that Mary might be in need, too. If she brought up her needs to him, he immediately counteracted with the needs of the other woman. Yet they both assured me that there was nothing going on there, and that they truly loved each other and wanted desperately to make this marriage work.

Mary had a good job with the state department and was financially responsible for not only all their bills together, she was also paying the house payment of the other woman each month and was filled with bitterness over it.

One afternoon I received an SOS phone call from Bob. He said Mary had been acting strange and had taken off work and for no apparent reason, was determined to drive in the pouring rain to Dallas (about 300 miles away). I tried to reach Mary, but she had already left, and all I could do was pray. I sensed somehow that she was desperate and had taken just about all that she could stand. The constant comparing of herself with the other women was more than she could handle, so we prayed and waited.

Three days later, we learned that Mary had pulled into a service station on her way to Dallas, gotten out of her car in the pouring rain, and laid down under the wheels of an eighteen-wheeler whose motor was already running. Someone who saw it jumped out of his vehicle and stopped the truck driver from starting up. They called the police who brought Mary back to San Antonio.

What could help this beautiful couple who constantly compared their present mates with their first ones? Or even themselves with each other? Only the Word of God could change them. There were other issues that needed attention too, but all their problems seemed to flow from the principle of their comparing with each other: her work with his (or his lack of work); her money with his; her friends with his; her church with his (or his lack of it)—on and on the list went.

Though it took months of the hammering of the Word, it was a joy to me, the way they both responded. They memorized 2 Corinthians 10:13:

For we dare not make ourselves of the number, or compare ourselves with some that commend themselves; but they measuring themselves by themselves and comparing themselves among themselves are not wise.

They also completed many assignments for me in the months we met together. I listed several things that they needed to do as priorities. One of these was to move away from Bob's first wife. No house, no matter how comfortable or nice, is to be compared with the importance of a relationship. I urged them to sell it and move away. Also I urged them to concentrate on choosing a church where they could both get involved and work in it together.

But underlying all the other details of their lives, we had to work to help them to totally break the habit of comparing— whether it was themselves to each other, or with others. This took several months of counseling, and a lot of changes. But the last time I saw them, they were happily working together in a good Bible-centered church and they told me that they had both been able to break the "comparing habit" by God's grace, and replace it with seven compliments a day.

6

Never Threaten

Knowing that whatsoever good thing any man doeth, the same shall he receive of the Lord, whether he be bond or free. And ye masters, do the same things unto them, forbearing threatening; knowing that your master is also in heaven; neither is there respect of persons with him.

(Ephesians 6:8-9)

It distresses me to hear parents threaten their children; even Christian parents who should know better, in light of Ephesians 6: 6-9. A young mother of two teenagers came to me one night at church, telling me how upset she was at her two children, and how she had threatened to put their clothes on the front porch and throw them out of the house. She boasted that she was doing the right thing. When I asked if she was aware of what Ephesians 6:9 says about threatening, she answered yes, but that she could not go on any longer. I pleaded with her to apologize to her children for threatening them and urged her to pray for reconciliation or things could get much worse if either of them moved out.

Obviously I didn't get through to her. The next week she told me her daughter had moved in with a married man. From there things went from bad to worse. These were teens who were raised in a Christian home. I couldn't begin to describe the tragedy and heartache that followed, including conflicts with the law.

Similar tragedies occur when threats are made within a marriage. A threat immediately sends you in opposite directions. This is never God's will. There's a difference between an understanding and a threat.

A threat gives the message that the issue at stake is more important than your spouse. This hurts and is demeaning. One of the most important elements in a *WOW* marriage is *loving trust*: a sense of totally belonging to each other and complete confidence in each other's love. A threat sends an opposite message and leaves deep wounds.

My husband and I were counseling a young couple once who seemed to have a wonderful marriage. But she had become uptight and her husband was baffled as to what to do. He knew he had hurt her, but she wouldn't tell him how.

Months later they had drifted far apart, and this beautiful Christian couple was bordering on divorce. They came for counsel but nothing surfaced. Finally, after much prodding, we learned that she had a quick temper, and sometimes in its heat, she lost control.

In one of these spats, he threatened to call the police, as she was losing it. She calmed down and it seemed to have healed over. But all those months, she carried a deep wound because of his threat. It made her doubt his love, and she thought their relationship was over.

God knows exactly what helps and what hurts human relationships. That threat from her beloved husband had been a sword in her heart, though she herself didn't know the cause of her hurt. As soon as they told us of the incident, we knew. He humbly apologized and healing came.

When our sons were young they sometimes used this as a challenge, if they didn't want to obey. "What will you do if I don't? Will you throw me out?" We used to answer, "No way. This home is yours until we put your hand into the hand of a godly wife in marriage. As for obedience, we will continue to command you, like Abraham did, and the decision then is yours, whether to please God by obeying, or otherwise." When God saw that the wickedness of Sodom was ripe for judgment, He said *"Shall I hide from Abraham that thing which I do? For I know him that he will command his children and his household after him, and they shall keep the way of the Lord to do justice and judgment"* (Genesis 18: 17, 19).

Refusing to threaten either as a parent or a spouse helps bring peace, security and trust. It cancels the need for arguments and resentments. God said simply that Abraham would "command" his children. That's all that's needed.

Threats are often the beginnings of violence. When one threatens, the other tries to outdo the first, and things go from bad to worse. Many couples who in the beginning don't really want a divorce, end up with one because they start down the road of threatening each other, which draws out the worst in each, and the little squabble escalates into war.

When one of our sons was in high school, two of his fine Christian friends came home with him on an obvious mission. I knew when they came in the front door that they had something controversial to persuade me about.

It was a time in our nation when high school students were going after the fad of renting an apartment. These three boys all had part-time jobs, and had figured out how much fun it would be to get an apartment together.

When they hit me with it, I prayed inwardly, knowing that our son was on the spot in front of his friends, and so was I. My thinking was, shall I postpone the answer? Shall I ask for time to pray about it? I knew in my spirit what the answer was already, so why prolong it and give them false hope?

My concern was our boy. He had been the ideal son—cooperative, dedicated to God, always communicative, and faithful—just a real joy. I didn't want to do anything to embarrass him, or hurt our relationship. Yet I knew that his life at that age was too precious to leave to chance. If ever a person needs the guidance of parents, it's in those middle teen years.

With great apprehension, I gave my answer: "Not on your life. Even if you're fifty years old before you marry, you're staying right here in this home." To my utter amazement, a great big grin spread on his face from ear to ear, as if to say with a big sigh of relief, "Wow! I didn't know you cared that much." And that was the end of it. Sure, the other boys were disappointed, but they needed to be home with their parents, too.

This son didn't marry until he was in his middle twenties, and we continued to command him, then left his response with God. This is so much better than threatening! It made for a beautiful relationship.

The principle of never threatening is vital to a *WOW* marriage. In our fifty-plus years, not once has either of us threatened to split, used the word divorce in relationship to us, or ever hinted that we wanted out. I am grateful for this. It would be hard to handle an up and down relationship and expect to be our best in ministering to troubled couples and all kinds of people who come for help and counsel.

It is wise however, to look at the difference between an understanding and a threat. In marriage there should be a clear understanding of what the other likes, desires, or disagrees with.

Some parents confuse threatening with a warning of what will bring punishment. The Bible clearly teaches that parents should discipline their children, even to the point that if we spare the rod we spoil the child. Punishment should not be thrown at a child in the form of a threat. It should be clearly defined on the child's level of understanding, so he knows that certain behaviors will produce the necessary punishment. It should not be the result of a parent's anger, but something the child earned and for which he is knowingly responsible.

When understandings are spelled out ahead of time, whether in parental relationships or in a marriage, this helps to avoid a lot of wounds, and cancels the seeming need to make threats. Threats usually come when the parties involved have not made proper plans about their goals and desires. Usually, when our goals are clearly set forward in any relationship, this brings understanding and the desire to work together to see those goals accomplished.

In a *WOW* marriage, this understanding is most important. Once when my husband was in ministry overseas, he had to call one of our church secretaries about business, and while he had her on the line, long distance, he asked her to relate to me that his arrival time had changed, and he gave her the information. I had no reason to be jealous of this lady, but in my spirit, I knew this wasn't right. As a rule, we try not to mix our personal lives with the public/ ministry arena, and I knew that we needed an understanding.

I didn't mention it when he got off the plane. But a few days later, while we were enjoying a lovely meal together I asked him if I was worth the $40 or so a phone call would have cost. His quick answer came with a puzzled look, "Of course, you are worth it!" he declared. Then I requested that from now on, even if it costs us extra, let's keep our personal lives away from the public view of our secretaries. Maybe that might be a bit much, but it has worked in a *WOW* way for over fifty years. I didn't threaten, nor was I pouting, but I felt that to protect our future, this was an understanding that our relationship needed.

Anytime something doesn't seem right in your spirit, you should take time to analyze it, pray over it, then hit it openly at a time when you are not rushed or under stress, and get the other's opinion on whether or not this should be dealt with in a particular way. Don't allow hazy questions to build distrust in your heart.

Remember, as married people, our first priority next to Jesus, is to guard our relationship to each other. If that breaks down, our ministry shrinks, our family is hurt, the kingdom of God is harmed, and our testimony is ruined. Though to threaten may seem like the logical thing to do in a moment of heat, it is hurtful, and should never be entered into.

Decide now, that you will never threaten each other, and you will keep principle number six for your *WOW* marriage.

Case in Point

Natalie had big brown eyes and dark curly hair and was in high school when I first met her. She was from a long line of pastors and she loved the ministry and was grateful for her godly heritage. She was a gifted girl with many visible talents—a lovely soloist and musician and had a warm, vibrant personality.

But she had one obvious weakness: a terrible sense of self-doubt, and to compensate, she used threats to get her way. Before she married, it was her mother and her friends whom she threatened. After her marriage to an evangelist, she tried to manipulate him with her threats to leave. Though the marriage continued for years, it was unstable. Even when the children came, there was turmoil and insecurity.

Though they were talented people, they were not able to stay with one ministry very long, because of her weakness. They had two beautiful daughters, very talented and popular at school. But they were following in their mother's steps, and had taken up the same habit of making threats in order to get their own way.

At her wit's end one day, Natalie called to say she had decided to end her life. She was suicidal and sounded dreadful on the phone. Years before when dealing with her in one of her despondent moods, I had made her promise to call if she was ever serious about giving up. The sobbing voice on the phone said: "I am a failure as a wife, a failure as a mother and a failure in ministry, so there is no use to try any longer." My heart began to race like crazy. What could I say to this dear friend who had lost all hope? Do you hit a person with their own weakness and fault when they are down that low? My impulse at a moment like this, is to be sympathetic, compassionate and tender—not condemning!

But as I silently prayed for help, The Holy Spirit said: "My knife and pruning is needed here."

"God," I whispered back, "She is already down on herself, enough to end it all. I don't want to push her down further." But God's still small voice was insistent, so I launched out.

"Natalie" I said, "Can I speak my heart to you? You are a beautiful lady, and you know I love you dearly, but when ever I think of you, I think of all the times you have used threats to get your way. Is this what you are doing now? Do you feel that by ending your life, or attempting to, that you are going to be able to manipulate circumstances?"

Silence. The long pause on the phone was making me antsy. Had I offended her? Had I made her already troubled spirit much worse? "O God," I cried inwardly, "Please, I need your wisdom." God is faithful when we remember to ask, and His wisdom is much higher than ours.

Finally she broke the silence. Sobbing, she told me how she didn't like the ministry they were involved in, and in spite of all she said or did, her husband was adamant that they were not going to move again. She had thought that suicide would somehow change all that—that if she began with me, it would get back to him, and then he would be willing to move on.

We prayed on the phone together, and a few weeks later Natalie came for a visit. We spent hours together checking out Scriptures—the importance of trusting God with our future and that when we use threatening to get our own way, this is the opposite to trust. At that time, her daughters were not serving the Lord and were getting more and more involved in the world. They had seen their mother get her way by threatening and they were following the same pattern. But when Natalie saw her mistake and repented, she returned home and seeing her own weakness reproduced in them, she began dealing with them about it, and asked them to also help her not to be guilty of it anymore.

Today the family is serving the Lord together in the same ministry where they have been for several years. There is a new security now about their family, since they have realized what the Bible says about threatening in Ephesians 6:9:

> *And ye masters, do the same things unto them, forbearing threatening; knowing that your Master also is in heaven; neither is there respect of persons with him.*

7

Never Say No

Giving thanks always for all things unto God and the Father in the name of our Lord Jesus Christ; submitting yourselves one to another in the fear of God. Wives, submit yourselves unto your own husbands, as unto the Lord.

(Ephesians 5:20-22)

When we understand what it means to submit to each other it becomes a joy to say "yes" each time our spouse makes a suggestion. This doesn't mean that we become weaklings or that we don't discuss our priorities or the wisdom of certain events that come up. But connecting the above verses together, this refusal to ever say no to your spouse comes from a heart of thanksgiving. Here, the Word says we are to be thankful for all things.

For years I was unaware of this verse. I had known the verse in 1 Thessalonians 5:18: "*In everything give thanks for this is the will of God in Christ Jesus concerning you*" (emphasis added). That is easy enough, for no matter what difficulty we face, God is still faithful—the unchanging One—so we can always give thanks in the midst of a problem. But *for* the problem? That's a different situation. And yet, that's what Ephesians 5:20 says—it even puts an extra "always" in there: "Giving thanks always *for* all things unto God." How can we give more emphasis to the difference between "*in* everything give thanks" and "*for* everything"?

Our phone rang one night in the wee hours of the morning. It was our older son in Iowa, sobbing on the other end. "My wife is suing for divorce, and I just don't want to live." He was suicidal.

Three children were involved, and we went to urgent prayer for them. Our desire was to see the marriage restored, but she had already given herself to another man. Our son's lawyer was sure that the children would be given to their mother, as that was the usual way in that state. It looked impossible, but we prayed and fasted.

During this time, the difference in the two verses above, with the two phrases "give thanks *for* all things" and "rejoice in all things" was quickened to us. God spoke clearly for us to rejoice for what was happening in our family.

I remember arguing with the Lord: how could I rejoice in a divorce when God hates divorce? Yet, there it was in the Word: "rejoice for all things." So in pure obedience, we began to thank the Lord for situations just as they were, divorce and all. In the middle of this battle, our son called to tell us of the miracle: the court had awarded the three children to him, and he had made a vow to always keep them in the house of God.

Something miraculous happens in the heavenlies when we give a sacrifice of praise, and rejoice in the Lord, regardless. Our son's attorney couldn't understand it. He said this never happens in Iowa, and yet it did. That was several years ago, and how God has worked in those three children. Two of them are in our Christian school, beautifully serving the Lord, and the oldest went to Bible College upon graduation.

It is this thankful heart, for all things just as they are, that gives us the joy to submit to one another. When we know God is in control, it is easy to always say yes. When we submit to each other, we are submitting to God.

If you practice this concept of never saying no to your mate, it will become a fun journey. In our marriage we've had some neat situations in relationship to this. When both partners try to practice this principle it sometimes gets really funny.

He'll come home and say, "Get ready, let's go out to eat." I'll say, "Okay sounds good," though down inside, I'm wishing we could have a cozy evening at home. Next thing I know, he's changed his mind. Here I've been getting ready, but he senses my spirit. We can go back and forth several times. We have lots of fun with this.

I remember one evening my husband called before coming home, suggesting we go for a swim together. I immediately answered "Okay let's go." But I had to teach that night and really wasn't in the mood for a swim and didn't want my hair to get messed up, but I put on my suit and waited. He didn't come home. Finally, an hour later he called to say someone in the church had an emergency and he was sorry to stand me up. (I was laughing inside because God had again taken care of it and I hadn't said no.) It is fun to submit to one another and trust the rest to God.

On another evening when I had to teach, Johnny called around 4:30 suggesting we go for a swim again. We swim at a nearby Holiday Inn, and usually at that time of day there is no one in the pool. Because we often put our guests in the Holiday Inn, the management allows us to freely use their pool whenever we please.

On this particular Tuesday, despite my love for swimming, it really wasn't my first choice, again, because I was to teach that night and knew what my hair looked like after an afternoon swim. But I determined to only say yes. So when Johnny called, I gave him an enthusiastic response. When we got to the pool, as usual, no one was in it.

But, after a few minutes a large group arrived—about 12 college kids, all from different states. They were in town for an academic convention of sorts. Suddenly our ears perked up as we became aware of their conversation. They were discussing various religions of the world, and it was obvious that none of them knew Jesus. It was our joy to swim over to them and tenderly enter their conversation. This released a barrage of questions about Christianity from the group. These young people were so open, they even allowed us to pray with them.

That evening we left the Holiday Inn with singing hearts. How glad I was that I had not said no! My teaching that night was enhanced by fresh joy and inspiration (and my hair didn't suffer, either).

Some wives have a problem with submission—it must be connected with a heart of thanksgiving. The Bible is not disjointed, and I love this connection. Though it is easier when both spouses are serving the Lord, submission can help an unsaved spouse to believe.

Ephesians 5:21 gives the balance. We wives are not the only ones to submit, it is a mutual submitting to each other in love. Scripture is clear on the headship of the man, (verse 23 and 1 Corinthians 11:1-3). Most ladies want their husband to be the leader. It gives covering and security in the big issues.

Daily decisions bring us into areas where we need to learn to never say no, as this is where disagreements arise. Saying yes must be preceded by a decision beforehand, and the key here is to do it with joy. This is another example of redeeming the situation before it happens.

Some couples get angry over what to eat, or what time to go to bed, or over what color curtains to buy. How God must laugh when He sees people make a mountain out of an ant hill.

One day, after we had returned from our honeymoon, my husband said to me jokingly: "You know, don't you, that you have to obey me in everything?" I answered very saucily: "Sure. And I will, as long as you do Ephesians 5:28, and love me as your own body." What a safeguard and balance the Scripture teaches.

Looking back on that now, I realize that is not really the way one should think. My submission to him should not be conditional on his behavior, but it should be according to the Word, for the Bible doesn't tell me to submit if—it just says to submit. My responsibility then is to obey and let God deal with him. This brings grace and enlargement.

It is not only the wife who is to submit. Ephesians 5:21 teaches us that submission is mutual: "*Submitting yourselves one to another in the fear of God.*" Putting that in modern words, it means to always say yes to each other. If we have been knowingly working on the first six principles of the *WOW* marriage, this principle of never saying no will come easily. I suggest that couples read Ephesians 5 together twice a year.

There are three safety valves that should never be violated when working on this principle of always saying yes to each other. Never violate: 1) God's Word, 2) your church's teaching, or 3) your conscience.

If we are to have a Christian marriage, it is imperative that we determine to obey the Word totally. Some couples are careful about this point but are careless in the other two, which creates problems. Every believer should have a good home church, know what the church teaches and be obedient to its teaching.

This cannot be violated even to please a spouse or to refrain from saying no. God's government is in His house and we must not violate His government. On the issue of the person's conscience, married couples must hold deep respect for the convictions of each other, even if they are not mutually held to the same degree.

This principle to never say no covers a large area of possible conflicts in a marriage, and prevents many misunderstandings when practiced consistently and deliberately. But *never* violate the aforementioned three principles, and be determined to always only strengthen your mate's convictions, even if you don't quite agree with them.

One Christmas evening, a husband wanted his wife to go out with him, just the two together. They had been with their families all day and he felt the need for their being alone together. A power struggle ensued, and with the excuse that they shouldn't leave their children, she took issue against him.

A big fight followed and neither the couple nor the children enjoyed the evening. There was yelling, accusations and tears, right in front of the children. What was the value in that? It would have been much better for the children to have been left with friends, than for them to have seen an awful fight between their parents. What a terrible way to end a lovely Christmas celebration.

Some wives try to be their husbands' conscience. This is not good. Each of us must stand or fall according to our own convictions and beliefs. The best thing for a wife to do when her husband is loose in his convictions, is to pray for him, and live a godly life of submission.

What recourse do we have when, in trying to always say yes, one spouse is loose about worldly things? That's where the three exceptions come in. It protects us—both husband and wife—when we consciously weigh everything with the question, "Does it violate 1) God's Word, 2) the teachings of our church, or 3) my conscience?"

One day a young husband flashed an excited look at me when he read my twelve point outline on the *WOW* marriage. This principle number seven especially caught his eye. He was a controlling young man and felt that at last he had someone who would take his side and allow him to dictate every detail in his wife's life. Some men have a "macho" attitude toward their wives. [Incidentally, the word *macho* comes from the root that means mule.] A *WOW* marriage has a balance in this area. This balance comes as both partners submit to each other joyfully. It comes two ways: 1) By both always saying yes, and 2) by moving through the first four principles (*Make Jesus Lord, Have an Ongoing Unselfishness Contest, Serve One Another Joyfully, and Refuse Strife and Criticisms*).

When you've worked through those four principles, plus the next two, this number seven will enlarge and enrich your wonderful *WOW* marriage. So decide now, to never, never say no!

Case in Point

Jim and Janie were Christians when they got married, but Janie knew she was taking a huge risk, for Jim loved to go drinking with his worldly friends and his dad was an alcoholic. But she told herself that with God's help she was positive she could change him. The years brought four little boys and multiplied problems. Jim was constantly buying new gadgets, getting drunk, disappearing for days at a time and never wanted them to pay their bills.

Janie was frequently harassed by bill collectors and nasty letters. All of her prayers, all of her appeals to Jim, and all of her efforts to keep their heads above water seemed useless. They were church people and Jim was a really likable guy, but through the years his drinking escalated and their bills mushroomed. What should Janie do?

When they came to the church for counseling, Jim's complaint was that Janie was an "evangelist." She was more interested in church and witnessing, and counseling her new converts on the phone by the hour than she was in him. He said this is what drove him to drink and to seek outside friends. Janie's complaint was that though they both had good jobs, it took all of her paycheck to keep the home and food for the family, while he blew his paycheck on booze and sports.

Besides all that, Janie was desperate to put their four boys in a Christian school, which meant added expenses. This is what finally drove them to seek for help.

Giving Jim Scriptures on drunkenness and the evils of liquor seemed to bounce off him like a ball. He was convinced that a beer or two wouldn't harm anyone. Appealing to Janie to submit to her husband only brought the response of verbal agreement. She claimed to already be submitting. But how could she treat Jim the same way she would treat the Lord Jesus, she asked, when most of the time he was bleary-eyed and hardly knew what he was doing?

"She never wants to do anything I want to do!" He blurted out in one of our sessions. "All she wants to do is go to church, go witnessing or go to foreign countries with mission teams. That's not my main interest. Why can't she go with me to places I want to go?"

"Do you want her to go drinking with you?" I asked.

"Oh no!" He exclaimed. "I'm glad she's such an evangelist. That's what attracted me to her. But, she never wants to go with me to ball games and sports events. She's a beautiful woman and I would like to show her off to my friends. Besides, our four boys are involved in a lot of things, and I'm constantly having to take them alone, because she always tells me 'no, not this time.' But it's that way all the time."

At that point, I drew the picture of the umbrella covering that Bill Gothard uses so effectively. It shows God at the top, in the shape of a diamond, the husband as an umbrella, the wife under its covering, while beneath the wife are the children. Neither of them had ever attended one of Gothard's Institutes in Basic Life Conflicts. With that drawing before them, I handed each of them a Bible and had them read Ephesians 5:20-22:

> *Giving thanks always for all things unto God and the Father in the name of our Lord Jesus Christ; submitting yourselves one to another in the fear of God. Wives, submit yourselves unto your own husbands, as unto the Lord.*

"How can I submit to him as unto the Lord, when he's such a hypocrite?" she began to sob. "I want more than life itself to please the Lord, but Jim's not interested in spiritual things."

I had to show her from several Scriptures that God's desire is that she do two things that are strongly evident in the above verse: 1) Be thankful for all things, (even for Jim as he is), and 2) submit to him in the fear of God.

When I shared with them how in fifty-plus years of our *WOW* marriage, we had practiced the principle of never telling each other no, both of them lit up. It was like the window shade in their heads had zoomed up! I had her turn to 1 Peter 3:1,2:

> *Likewise ye wives, be in subjection to your own husbands; that, if any obey not the word, they also may without the word be won by the conversation of the wives; While they behold your chaste conversation coupled with fear.*

I explained that in the modern vernacular, that means "NEVER SAY NO!" Of course I gave them the three biblical exceptions:

1. Never violate the commands of Scripture.
2. Never violate the teachings of your church.
3. Never violate each other's conscience.

As the weeks passed and this principle became a foundation for them, Jim and Janie began to change. She went everywhere with him (except to the bars) and he came with her to church. It didn't happen overnight, but gradually God's grace became evident in their lives. His drinking became less and less, they began to pay their bills, and today, their children are in our Christian School.

8

Practice Humor

*When the Lord turned again the captivity of Zion
we were like them that dream. Then was our mouth filled
with laughter, and our tongue with singing; then said
they among the heathen, the Lord hath done great things
for them.*

(Psalms 126:1-2)

My parents were missionaries in Japan. As a little girl
growing up in Japan, I used to dream about being married
to a godly man, and how we would be lovey-dovey all our
lives. Every girl has similar dreams. (When we got married,
the captivity of my singleness was turned, and like the verse
above, I was like those who dream.) There has always been
a lot of laughter in our home, and it helps break tensions.
During the fifties and sixties, Johnny and I spent six years
as missionaries in Japan, planting churches in new towns.

Having grown up in Asia my life was enriched with a lot of funny tales. Daddy used to tell how when he first began preaching in Japanese he preached a whole sermon to a crowded tent on *charcoal*—thinking he was preaching on *sin*. The only difference was he dropped the needed *T*. Sin in Japanese is *tsumi*, while charcoal is *sumi*. Another point of laughter was when one of the newly arrived missionaries sang a beautiful song to a crowded church thinking she was singing "Grace, Grace, God's Grace." She actually sang, "Rat, Rat, God's Rat." Grace in Japanese is *megumi*, while rat is *nezumi*.

Another incident that brought a big laugh to our family was the missionary who learned just two phrases in Japanese when he first arrived: *Gochisosama* (meaning "it was a feast") and *Arigato* (which means "thank you"). Eager to make his acquaintance, the little Japanese boy next door gave them one of his kittens. The next time the missionary saw the little boy, trying to be polite and intending to be saying thank you, he got the two phrases mixed, and said *Gochisosama* ("it was a feast"). The poor little boy ran into his house crying, "Mama! Mama! That foreigner ate my kitten."

Christians have more fun than anyone. The idea that you have to be long-faced to be spiritual is hogwash. There are a lot of little sayings we have between us that are our own little jokes. Families can do this with a lot of situations and add spice and laughter.

Work can be made fun. Eating should be fun, spending time together should be filled with laughter, joy and love.

Sex should be fun. Prayer should be fun. The Bible should be pure joy; it is God's great Word to us. But it's up to us as couples to get this perspective. The Bible says God laughs and there are numerous incidents in Scripture that point to His obvious sense of humor. This is something we need to work on and develop in our homes.

Our verse at the beginning of this chapter connects laughter with singing. One of the fondest memories of my childhood is my mother going about her work singing. Though she didn't sing solos at church, her songs at home brought brightness and joy. She also laughed a lot. I have wonderful memories of my childhood—lots of singing and lots of laughter. When I was a girl, Mother used to awaken us with little jingles—some with spiritual truths woven into them, and some were just plain funny. I guess I inherited that from her, as I often sing little jingles to our grandchildren when they come to visit and need to be roused from their beds. One of my favorites is:

"Birdie with a yellow bill, hopped upon my window sill,

Cocked his shining eyes and said, 'Aren't you ashamed, you sleepy-head?

Aren't you ashamed you're still in bed?' "

Little jingles sung or spoken add spice, especially when they are songs and jingles of love and compliments. The first time Johnny told me he loved me, he did it by singing to me: "Let me call you sweetheart, I'm in love with you."

Though that was many years ago, it is just as fresh in my memory today—as if it were yesterday. Singing soothes the soul, and lifts the spirit. Fill your home with laughter, music, and song. There's nothing like it.

Sing your praises to God, and let Him give you new songs by His Spirit. This will wash away some of the garbage that comes in through life. Obviously God loves new songs, for Scripture (especially Psalms) is filled with the command for us to "*sing a new song unto the Lord.*" A little boy wrote President Nixon when he was in office, asking what it would take for him to become the president of the United States.

President Nixon wrote back and told him to do three things: 1) Learn all you can, 2) love all you can, and 3) laugh all you can.

The Bible says that laughter does good like a medicine and by deliberately focusing our lives on laughter, we can add a dimension of joy to our surroundings. Do you ever laugh out loud? Try it often, it will bless you and those around you. It is sad when people never laugh.

Sometimes married people are too serious, especially when there are many cute little intimate things to laugh together about. What about when one of you is overly tired and a bit grouchy? Try a bit of humor and break the tension. We need to throw back our heads and laugh, instead of letting little stupid things irritate us. Two of our dear friends, a minister and his wife, giggle at everything. They are an older couple, and always, when we meet them at the airport, they come down the ramp giggling. They are a tonic to be around. This oils the hinges of life. Why are we so serious?

One Christmas, our family was gathered around the tree loaded with gifts. It is our tradition to read the Christmas story and pray together before we open gifts. The room was crowded and several of the ladies were trying to gather chairs around for everyone to sit on.

During the confusion, someone was taking pictures with the camcorder when his wife got in his way, triggering a stern rebuke. Instead of handing back a sharp retort (which would be a normal response), she ran to him, threw her arms about him and laughed, saying, "I love you honey, and will not let you get tensed up." That broke the tension, and soon he was laughing too.

By responding to anger with humor, you redeem the situation ahead of time. You decide to instantly forgive when something like that happens. It is the same principle that enables you to apologize when you are falsely accused and you know there is no basis for the other's anger. We don't have to defend ourselves when someone is irritated. The moment you defend yourself, you make the other person your judge. If you refuse to defend yourself, that makes God your defense, and He becomes the judge. How wonderful that is. Instead of getting uptight, you can stand there and smile.

We have a king-size bed, and frequently my husband lends a hand and helps me to make it up, as otherwise, it takes several trips around it back and forth. I don't expect him to do this, and never ask for his help unless I'm in a bind time-wise, but when we do it together there are a lot of cute little private jokes shared and laughed over. This is humor even in the little routines of life.

God wants your marriage to be fun. He wants you to enjoy each other—celebrate each other. We have a crazy thing in our family. It's a rolled-up ball of string covered with adhesive tape. Each Christmas or birthday, whoever got it last, is supposed to wrap it up in a big box and give it as a gift. We write dates on it. It's just a fun thing that we do, and for some reason, we all forget who had it last. In fact, right now I don't know which family has it.

One night after church, the two of us got the giggles over an evangelist from Canada who was staying with us. He had gone out with friends for a bite to eat after the service, and we had left the front door open and the living room light on. It was late when he came in, but we were still awake, and lay there listening to him locking the front door, turning off the lights, and stumbling into the dark hall and bathroom.

He had never stayed in our home before, and didn't know that we keep a tape player turned on with the light switch in our front bathroom. He was tiptoeing, trying to be quiet. We heard him gently shut the bathroom door and when he turned on the light, a man's voice came out of the tape player—Alexander Scourby was reading the Scripture—at the very place where it said, "Ha! Ha!" (Job 39:25).

The poor preacher was startled and we heard him fumble as he struggled to turn the tape player off. Unknown to him, we were both lying in bed splitting our sides with laughter. We all had a good laugh over it the next morning.

We've had a lot to laugh about in our marriage, especially when circumstances create tension. Once when we were singing a duet on the radio, we were holding two song books, one atop the other, because our song was to be followed by another song from a different book. Wouldn't you know it, right while we were singing the song from the top book, somehow that book slid down and, with a resounding "plop!" landed on the floor. We both got the giggles and couldn't finish the song. But prince of preachers that Johnny is, he turned it into humor and told the radio audience what a happy life it is to serve the Lord, and that even when a book drops in the middle of a special number, we can laugh and praise the Lord.

Mother often sang the little jingle: *"Laugh and the world laughs with you. Weep, and you weep alone."* If you want to bless your partner, get the laughing habit. But beware of humor at someone else's expense. Laughter or humor that hurts another person is always wrong. But laughing at yourself or negative circumstances lifts your spirit and lets the sunshine in.

My Dad often quoted "Faith laughs at impossibilities and cries 'It shall be done!' " This was an exciting boost to my faith. Humor and laughter permeate the boring and humdrum life with color and excitement. The Christian life has no room for a "pity party." As a girl, it distressed me that Jesus rebuked Peter and even called him Satan when Peter remonstrated over Jesus' coming death (see Matthew

16:22-23). But in the margin of my Bible it says that Peter actually said, "Pity you." When I saw that, I realized it was that negative root of self-pity that Jesus was rebuking.

God wants us to abound with blessings and joy. So throw back your head and laugh! Laugh when you're lonely, laugh when you goof up, laugh when you're broke. God laughs—so should you!

Refusing self-pity, and laughing at your situation instead, will enable you to obey God's call in your life and help you to overcome any resistance to the Holy Spirit you might have struggled with, thereby allowing you to do God's will with abounding joy!

With just a little forethought, you can add lots of laughter to your marriage. The more you put into it, the more fun it will be. So step number eight towards a *WOW* marriage is practice humor.

Case in Point

"Can I still be a Sunday School teacher even if I divorce my husband?" Susan asked one day in a counseling session. Her husband, Bill, was an attorney and a truly fine man, but his work nearly consumed him, and he only attended church at Christmas and Easter. Susan had seriously considered leaving him for the past two years, and I was struggling to try and help her hang in there.

I knew it was hard for her to serve the Lord alone—coming to church alone all the time. Bill's whole focus was work and money. Their home was beautiful, but it was sad and empty. Everything was too serious—there was no laughter and no joy.

One day Susan told me that God had given her a brand new song while she was doing the dishes. But when Bill came home and she sang it to him, he scorned it. Though it was about the Lord, it was a sad song, and rather mournful. God used that song to open my eyes to Susan's real problem: She was too serious about everything.

So we began working on humor. I told her that Bill didn't need a sermon when he came home from work—he needed laughter and relaxation. Nowhere in the Bible are we taught to be sad and long-faced. Instead, we are commanded over and over to REJOICE! Paul said in Philippians 4:4: *"Rejoice in the Lord alway; and again I say rejoice."*

People have the mistaken idea that to be spiritual, they have to be sad. That is not biblical at all. Nehemiah 8:10 says, *"The joy of the Lord is our strength."* Together, Susan and I went over a lot of the Scriptures on joy and rejoicing, until she was convinced of her need to begin laughing out loud and filling her home with praises to God. I told her that as she formed the habit of setting her will to be a praiser, creative ideas would come to her for little fun things in their marriage that would help bring back the sparkle and excitement they had in the beginning.

God was faithful to give her all sorts of ideas. She began by fixing candlelight dinners—even when Bill came home late. At his plate she placed artistic, funny little poems that described her heart for him, or his responses. (Nothing pointedly religious.) She began practicing laughing out aloud—not a "horse" laugh, but genuine laughter. She looked for cute jokes about marriage and love which she shared with him. When he was tired and short-tempered with her, she rushed to him and threw her arms around him, laughingly telling him how wonderful he was.

She stuck little notes in his pajamas. She placed little notes in his briefcase (which sometimes he would discover just as he stood up to speak in a court trial). He began coming home earlier. He would call and ask her out to dinner more frequently. He began sharing with her about some of the cases he was handling at work, whereas before she was entirely left out of his life.

Suddenly they realized they had rediscovered each other. They both began to laugh a lot and genuinely enjoyed being together. And he began going to church with her—not every Sunday, but now and then. For some reason he enjoyed the Sunday night services the most, so I encouraged her to work with him on this even if it meant skipping the other services to come with him. I knew God was at work and it was only a matter of time before God's grace would draw Bill in.

What a day of rejoicing it was when Bill went forward to receive Christ as Savior. What for years looked like an impossibility was now a reality. But I had to caution Susan to not let up on her determination to practice humor. Satan will always try to get us focused on the negatives in life. Scripture is strong in reinforcing the positive.

Remember that it is not the circumstances in life that determine our joy or sadness, it is the set of the will to REJOICE!

9

Honor and Respect

Be kindly affectioned one to another with brotherly love; in honor preferring one another.

(Romans 12:10)

I once heard a psychologist say, "Honor is the most important word in the English language." How different homes would be if married couples were to always honor each other. Our verse above says to prefer one another with honor. What a wonderful goal.

In Ephesians 5:33, Paul goes one better yet. He says: *"Let everyone of you in particular so love his wife even as himself; and the wife see that she reverence her husband."*

How would your spouse feel if every time he came home you went "Wow!" as he walked in the door? Wouldn't that ignite the atmosphere? Or what if you looked at each other with awe? Gary Smalley says couples should actually do this, actually say "Awe! Wow!"

Whether we verbalize it or not, if we could discipline ourselves to keep this attitude toward each other it would do wonders for our relationship. This is why we are strong on daily giving each other at least seven compliments. When we do, it magnifies the good in the other instead of focussing on their flaws. It oils the hinges and makes life smoother.

Not only should we honor and respect each other's person and his desires, we also must honor our marriage vows. Neglect in this area can make us careless in our association with the opposite sex.

Scripture has multiple warnings against adultery and fornication. Proverbs 6:32,33 says it brings a deep wound, and destroys the soul (puts scars on our emotions). It brings dishonor, and its reproach will not be removed.

Eggs can never be unscrambled, and an adulterous situation even when forgiven, is hard to overcome. The full relationship of the past is rarely restored completely. Hurtful memories are hard to erase. There's a difference in flirting and being friendly.

A Christian should never flirt, and should be discreet in all associations. The Bible says to avoid the appearance of evil and this includes avoiding situations that might become questionable. One such situation is when a person goes to lunch with someone of the opposite sex alone or becomes involved in personal problems or counseling.

My husband and I have a standing rule that neither of us will ever counsel anyone of the opposite sex alone. We also have this rule for our church staff. Counseling is a very intimate area, and to do it alone with the opposite sex is playing with fire.

Just because you are a Christian doesn't mean that you are not vulnerable. If the great King David, with all his love for God and his hours of worship could fail in this area, so can any one of us. We must guard our marriage with wisdom and avoid Satan's traps, for they are there.

Jesus said that if a man looks lustfully at a woman he has already committed adultery in his heart (Matthew 5:28). Solomon, in describing the virtuous woman, declared that she will always do her husband good and not evil and he can safely trust her. A good marriage must be built on trust, and trust in this area comes through honor and respect.

Not only are we to honor each other, but self-respect is vitally important. When a person begins to dabble with pornography, or cheap books and magazines, it is because he has lost self-respect, and no longer honors his own person as created in the image of God. This honor toward oneself is important.

When I have the radio on, even on a Christian station, if they start singing a "poor me" type song, I turn it off. I don't want to imbibe that type of music into my spirit. This is not wrongful pride, it is standing for our sacred position as temples of the Holy Ghost.

Lack of this kind of honor and self-respect frequently brings problems into marriage because one partner allows the other to trample him under foot. God never intended this. We are partners in marriage, heirs of the kingdom of God. The wise way is to confront a hurtful situation when it first surfaces, as sometimes we can hurt each other without intending to and are not aware of the results.

If your mate wounds you find out if he is aware of it. Show him that you are not jealous but that you feel it is important that you honor each other.

One area of irritation for me is when I fix a lovely hot meal and my husband comes home hours late—the food is cold and I am hot. It has been a struggle of mine for years. I sometimes rise above it and can smile in spite of the ruined meal, but sometimes I clam up and feel wounded, and I hate myself when I do this. I feel I am at least due the honor of a phone call. What I should do is throw my head back and laugh!

In the ministry all kinds of emergencies arise in people's lives and sometimes the urgent takes preeminence over the important. We have to sort out these two principles frequently. The Lord has dealt with me about this and thank God I've improved some. God gives grace even in these situations.

Not only should we honor each other's expectations and time, but also their workload and limitations. This is part of being unselfish, as well as honoring each other. As married couples, we need to stay on our toes all the time lest our relationship become commonplace and we begin to take each other for granted. How would you honor the Lord Jesus if He walked into your house? Oh, that we would honor our mates with the same level of respect. When the wife truly makes her husband the "king of his castle" that automatically makes her the queen.

There are many practical ways we can honor our spouse, especially our husband, and I will list a few of them here:

1. **Don't be a controller.** Some women, as soon as they are in the car with their husband, begin telling them where to turn, how to drive, etc. This drives him up a wall! When I've been guilty of this, my husband has sometimes asked, "How do you think I drive all the time when you're not along?" Always wanting to control conveys a lack of trust. Total trust brings with it honor and respect.

2. **Don't disdain his achievements.** Whatever your spouse does, lavish praise should be the norm. Whether it is baking cookies (with a big mess left in the kitchen), mowing the lawn, or preaching a sermon, honor your mate with thankfulness and appreciation (without any

"buts" or comparisons with someone else's achievement.)

3. **Always be on your mate's side.** When we side with a critic, this is disloyal and dishonoring to our beloved. If the criticism is valid or has some truth to it, it is not honoring the relationship if we push the knife in deeper when we have been taken into his confidence. Honoring our mate means we are always on his or her side, regardless of the circumstance or accusation. If a situation needs to be dealt with, it is wise to wait until a later time, and not right when someone has "spilled his guts" to us. It is most important as "one flesh" people, that we always display honor to each other and stand together as one. We must always show caring understanding (not condemnation) when he or she is hurting.

4. **Don't nag.** The wise man said, *"It is better to live in a corner of a house top than to live in a palace with a brawling woman."* A couple came to us who worked opposite shifts and seldom saw each other. Though they had had a good marriage in the past, they had become estranged and he wanted out. Several children were involved and she was willing to fight for her marriage. They were both Christians and there was no apparent infidelity, but we learned that she constantly nagged him because he didn't come straight home from work. He would go out to eat with friends after work, and this made her furious. The few minutes in the mornings when they saw each other, it was nag, nag, nag. We told her she should get up in the night (around 2 A.M.), fix him a lovely meal, and sit there and fellowship with him while he unwound. Since he had a weird schedule due to his work, she could go to bed earlier and set the alarm clock in order to meet his needs. When she agreed to do this, she stopped nagging, and he began to come to church.

Instead of honor and respect, many couples see each other's flaws and constantly pick at them. This is not honor. In Jesus' prayer to His Father in John 17:10, He said He was glorified in His disciples. Can you imagine being glorified in such flawed men as Judas the betrayer, Peter who denied Him, and doubting Thomas? If Jesus could honor these men to the point of being glorified in them, we can surely give honor and respect to the one with whom we have become one flesh.

Put down your own soulish man who wants to argue against God's higher standard of honor. Your soul wants to lift you up in pride and give you a hard, stubborn heart. David asked several times, *"Why art thou cast down, O my soul?"* (Psalms 42:5, 11; 43:5). This showed his conflict between his soulish man and his spirit. This is where we often struggle also.

Learn to recognize the origin of your thoughts and secret conversations with yourself. All thoughts are from one of three sources: the Holy Spirit (who always agrees with the Word); the devil; or your soul. Since the soul wars against the Spirit, learn to squash your arguing, soulish man and obey the Spirit. This begins in your mind by your agreement with the Word.

As your mind is aligned with the Word, this releases the Spirit to take control. As this happens, it becomes easier to honor your mate, even if things are negative. Alignment with the Word and the Spirit is a powerful tool for helping you to genuinely honor your partner with all your heart.

Jesus never put needy people down. He honored them with compassion and forgiveness; even the woman of Samaria who had had 5 husbands and was in an immoral relationship; even the woman taken in adultery whom the men of the city wanted to stone. Jesus lifted her up with forgiveness and honor by saying, *"Neither do I condemn thee: go and sin no more"* (John 8:11).

During my last year in Bible college, a situation came up that distressed me to the point that I wanted to go home, forgetting my diploma. I didn't know what to do. I felt the school had been unjust and I was ready to leave. I called my parents for counsel, and will never forget the honor they gave me. They told me they would be praying, and that they had total confidence that I would find God's will and walk in it, regardless of the diploma; that doing God's will was the most important thing. Their honor and trust sent me to my knees, and instead of dropping out of school I stayed, took the discipline, and graduated with joy, all because of my parent's honor.

Ephesians 6:2 says we should honor our parents and that if we do, we are promised a good and long life. Parents in a home represent the government of that home, thus in honoring parents the authority issue is being clearly defined. When a couple gets married they must understand that they are establishing the government of a new home. This is why it is important that Christians marry only Christians. They are about to establish the government of a new home and family.

Within this issue of honoring each other there are three basics that each couple should be aware of:

1. Headship (Government)
2. Heartship (Love overflowing in all areas)
3. Hopeship (Vision and goals for the future)

Two heads make a monster, and each couple needs to see the biblical principle of the headship of the man as the leader of this new government and work within that framework to bring order and peace without infringement. Small children are sensitive to this issue, to such a degree that when a mother goes to the baby-sitter to pick up her child, suddenly the toddler who has behaved well all day begins to act up. The baby-sitter will say "He was good until you walked in." What happened here? The young child knew he was in the presence of two authorities and a monster emerged. Two heads make a monster.

The heartship principle is based on relationship. This brings with it the responsibility to not only honor each other, but be willing to be vulnerable and open. All facades and hypocrisy must go.

The third issue is important for forming goals and vision. I used to wonder why they put Samson's eyes out after they cut his hair and he no longer had any strength. Then I realized that his eyes spoke of vision. They knew that without his eyes even if his hair grew back and his strength returned, a blind man can't do much against the enemy. In Samson's case, his spiritual sight returned, his anointing of the past was renewed, and when he felt his hair begin to grow he knew that his strength had returned. With renewed vision and new strength he killed more enemies in his death than in his life.

Scripture says that people perish without vision. How important it is in our marriages to have vision and goals for the future. As we honor each other in our *WOW* marriage, we need to do so within the confines of these three important basics: Government, Heart, and Vision. What would happen to children if parents would remember this principle more often? I remember when we were growing up how strict our daddy was that we never talk back to mother, or to our older sister. This was never allowed for it would dishonor them. If this were practiced more today, it would solve many misunderstandings, especially with teenagers.

Honor is one of the greatest needs in the life of a teen; not only do they need to learn to honor others, they themselves need to be honored by their parents and siblings.

That being the case let's begin it in our marriage. What a principle this number nine is: *"In honor preferring one another!"*

On a recent ministry trip to Japan, one of the churches there asked me to minister on biblical principles for a good marriage. When the issue of honoring one another came up, and we turned to Romans 12:10, the audience acted stunned. It became obvious that many of the men had never heard that truth, and after the service, they asked a lot of questions about it. One pastor gasped: "Me honor my wife?"

Years ago in the Orient women were considered personal property. The idea of giving them honor was unthinkable. But the Bible is clear that we are to honor each other—both young and old, male and female. What a difference this makes in personal relationships.

When my husband and I were missionaries in Japan, it fell to me to teach the young pastors' wives to give public affirmation to their husbands. This was hard for them, as the Japanese culture is such that you should always put down those who are related to you and make negative remarks about them. If someone complimented the husband's sermon, their first response would naturally be: "No it wasn't good at all." They had to be taught that the Bible is not Eastern or Western in culture, but Christian, and the Christian way is to speak highly of one another and not cut each other down.

One of the best ways to have God's Spirit working freely in your marriage is to honor one another. Jesus said, *"Whatsoever ye do to the least of these, ye do it unto me."*

Number nine then of our twelve *WOW* principles is: *"In honor prefer one another."* Begin today to honor your mate in the same way as you would the Lord Jesus if He were to physically walk into your house.

Case in Point

Tim was a new Christian and the joy of the Lord oozed out of him constantly. He came early to every service and to Early Morning Prayer at 6 a.m. He was a dentist and had a beautiful family of two boys and two girls. His children loved the church, but his wife Diane refused to come. She said she didn't like Tim "religious" and wished he'd go back to the man he was before.

She would rather have him staying out late and coming home drunk. She had pleasant memories of their Sunday picnics together, or lazy Sunday mornings when they slept in and the paper was sprawled all over the bedroom. Now he was always gone on Sundays, and when he was home, all he wanted to do was read the Bible or listen to gospel music. She was sick of it and wanted out.

How do you tell a man to stop being a fanatic lest he lose his family? God's Word tells us to be wholehearted in serving the Lord, yet how do we balance this with the emotional needs of members of our family who are not there yet? I believe Romans 12:10 is the answer:

> *Be kindly affectioned one to another with brotherly love; in honor preferring one another.*

Tim was finally able to convince Diane to come (reluctantly) to counseling. I could tell immediately that she was weary of Tim's extreme devotion to the Lord and His kingdom. She was upset over the $1,000 he had given to provide Bibles to China, of the monthly missions pledges he had made, and countless other gifts he had contributed to the church. She felt rejected and neglected and was jealous of his time and attention. At one point in our first session she blurted out, "If he'd only go to another church, I'd go with him and might even get saved myself!"

I asked Tim if he'd ever thought about the importance of honoring his wife and preferring her desires above his own. He gave me a blank look, like he didn't understand.

"How would you treat Diane if she were Jesus Christ?" I asked.

"Oh," he said, "that would be different. I would gladly do anything He asked."

And so began a lengthy series of counseling sessions based on the principle of honoring and respecting each other. It had to be a two-way street. Not only did Tim have to do some changing, but Diane had to also.

For Diane to even consider going to church anywhere was a big step for her. So slowly and gently, I suggested they visit some churches together. Throughout this process, my one concern was the danger of uprooting their children who loved our church. But this is where faith had to work. I knew that nothing can be worse than a family breaking up, so we proceeded on the importance of honoring one another and respecting their desires.

One Saturday a phone call came from Tim. "What shall I do?" he asked. "Diane wants to go to this very dead, formal church that I just can't stand. Should I honor her desire and go along, or shall I keep doing what I enjoy? And what should I do about the kids?"

The Holy Spirit instantly gave me an answer. This would possibly be only temporary; that Diane was probably testing his new decision to honor her—so he should go along with it, even for several weeks. Who knows? God can even work in a dead formal place. His grace is never limited to locations. And as for the children, since we were believing it was a temporary arrangement, why not drop them off at the church they loved, and let them be with their friends in Sunday School?

Tim's decision to honor his wife was not only in the religious arena. It began to spill over into their finances, their time together and their goals for their children. After he went to church with her four times, she decided she didn't like that church either, and quit going. Now what should Tim do? I suggested he give a little more; stay home with her one Sunday if she would agree to come with him the next. This too, we believed would be only temporary, but it would be a vital part of his giving her honor and respect.

At first Diane took advantage of Tim's desire to honor her, but gradually, a change took place. She began to reciprocate. She began doing little things to honor him that she had never done before. All this time I had reminded them to give each other seven compliments a day, and they were both trying hard to do this. I asked them each to bring a list of the compliments they gave to each other to the counseling sessions.

For about three months, Diane came to church with Tim and the children every other Sunday. Then it happened! In one of our counseling sessions she broke completely down and said she was tired of her selfishness; tired of rebelling against God, and could I help her get right?

We got on our knees, and right in my office, Diane surrendered her life to the Lord. When we got up off our knees, it was beautiful! Tears of joy were splattering everywhere as they hugged each other. Now they would not have to "force" their honor and respect for each other, but as truly one flesh, in spirit soul and body, they would joyfully honor one another as part of the family of God.

10

Give Each Other Space

*Set me as a seal upon thy heart, as a seal upon
thine arm; for love is strong as death, and jealousy is
cruel as the grave, the coals thereof are coals of fire,
which hath a most vehement flame.*

(Song of Solomon 8:6)

A common difficulty in some marriages, especially
when the wife is home all day is when one mate smothers
the other. When the husband comes home she wants to know
every detail of his day. While he's eager to get home and
relax she's eager to talk, wanting him to show interest in
her day. It is said that women say 25,000 words a day while
the average man says only 10,000.

By the time he gets home he is talked out and she's
just ready to begin. If there are small children, she is likely

tired of baby talk and is ready for communicating on a higher level. His apparent lack of excitement about her and the kids can bring misunderstanding and wounds.

She is probably not aware of it, but the danger here is distrust, and some jealousy may be at the root. She has probably never consciously made space for him in their relationship and is thinking mainly about her own needs, not his.

Frequently we hear the cry from young wives or mothers, "My husband doesn't talk to me. Doesn't share with me. I feel left out of his life, all alone." Some say this is because women talk more than men. Possibly that is part of it, but whatever the cause, a quality decision on the part of each to give space to the other helps overcome this problem.

Give each other space and avoid the temptation to smother your spouse. Accept him as he is. Don't breathe down his back all the time. Don't try to be his conscience. Let him make his own decisions.

Don't mother him. You're his wife and sweetheart, not his mother. Don't let him call you mother, just because the kids do. In our relationship, we never call each other mom or dad unless we're talking to our sons. If one of us slips on this the other will quickly bring correction. "I'm not your dad" or "I'm not your mom."

Let your spouse have his or her own friends, own hobbies and some occasional time away from you without your feeling abandoned. Let him or her feel free, not controlled by you.

As a pastor's wife, I must make room for my husband to spend large segments of time doing his radio ministry, sermon preparation, counseling people's needs at all hours, hospital ministry, Bible study and preparation for weddings and funerals.

On top of all this, he tries to find one day a week to play golf. At first I resented this. His only day off was at the golf links, and I wasn't included (by my own choice). People have asked if this doesn't bother me. Not any more, for the years have taught us that if we give each other space then the times we are together are more special.

It's good to hang loose in this area. If he wants to read or work on his notes, I busy myself with stuff I want to do. My first desire is that he can relax at home and feel free to do whatever he needs to do without me pouting or accusing him of neglect.

There are some weeks that we're both home for lunch every day; then there are others when one of us is going to luncheons with other people, or committee meetings and we rarely see each other. He's often gone at breakfast to various kinds of leadership breakfasts, elders' breakfasts, and citywide pastors' prayer breakfasts.

Sometimes these events which cause us to go our separate ways seem to bunch together, but we know that's only temporary and we'll be back to normal soon. This is trust and trust is vital for a *WOW* marriage.

I'm not big on sports except for swimming. My husband loves it all. He is a better husband when he gets the proper exercise. Now I encourage him to play golf and racketball or whatever. I'm glad for him to have his own friends for these outlets. They help break the tensions of the ministry and might even save his life.

A lady warned me once that I should frown on my husband going to the racketball club. Didn't I know there is a lot of evil in those places and he might fall into temptation? And people gamble over their golf games. There's potential evil everywhere you go and people can gamble over anything, even the weather. Giving each other space is letting go of fears and distrust. We must trust each other, and give each other space.

My husband encourages me to get together with my friends from high school and college days. He likes for me to go to lunch with my friends or be involved with political groups, and never have I known him to try to hold me back or limit my outside activities unless he sees I'm getting physically or mentally tired. That's the only time he steps in and it is obvious he's doing it for my protection. I really appreciate this. Both the space he gives and the protection he provides tell me that he really loves me. Ephesians 5:23 says the husband is the savior of his wife's body.

What about jealousy? How should we handle it? If it's in you, squash it! The best way to overcome jealousy is to make a quality decision to not allow it in your heart for a moment.

Just as you make the decision to submit to each other you do the same with jealousy when it tries to arise.

Jealousy is the fear of being replaced by another. If you and your mate are nurturing your love and are practicing the ten principles for a *WOW* marriage we've discussed, there should never be a jealous bone in your body or in your relationship.

Before we married, when I realized we would be in the ministry and involved with all kinds of people, I made some quality decisions. One was to submit to my husband. Another was to forgive instantly. And another was to never be jealous. This doesn't mean we're to be naive. If it should become obvious that some lady or man is overstepping discreet boundaries, go after him or her (kindly, of course).

There have been a few times in our marriage when it became obvious that someone seemed too interested in my husband. When that has happened, I've cautioned him to be alert. Men are quite adept at freezing out someone who is trying to get intimate and Johnny is no exception.

We both practice strict discipline on ourselves and we teach others likewise: never go out to lunch alone with someone of the opposite sex; never counsel someone of the opposite sex alone; never be in the house alone with someone of the opposite sex unless it's a repairman.

I don't invite our male neighbors into the house if they show up at our door, or if one of the church men come by I talk to them on the front porch where all the world can see what's going on. Not that we don't trust others; we have two important areas of life to give first priority protection: our testimony, and our marriage.

No third person can slip in and get the advantage. These precautions help build trust and enable us to freely give each other space. A time or two, new baby Christians have fallen in love with my husband. I remember him bringing me a love letter that one of them wrote him. It was quite intimate and mushy. He handed it to me saying, "Read this, then you must deal with it."

It was from a lady about our age whom he had led to the Lord at the altar and had baptized her and her husband in water. I laughed when I read it, but felt sorry for her for I knew she had confused her love for Jesus with a sense of physical love for my husband. I was glad that I didn't feel the slightest tinge of jealousy or resentment.

I prayed about how to handle it. We'll call her Freida, though that is not her name. When she heard my voice on the phone she gasped, "Oh no! Are you terribly mad at me for being in love with your husband?" "No" I said, "You're not in love with my husband at all. You're in love with Jesus and because my husband is the one who led you to the Lord, you have your emotions mixed up."

She was sweet yet fearful. I had to work to convince her that because of her past life being so focused on the physical and because her environment had always made sensual issues dominant, she had fallen into that kind of a trap with her emotions focused on Pastor. I told her how she should close that door and open her emotions to Jesus and this would eclipse all those guilt feelings and fears.

It was wonderful how the Lord handled that situation. There was no fracture or strain in any of our relationships and God worked it out. Even her husband understood and there was no more problem.

What should you do when your husband is jealous of you? Some wives can't stop at the store on the way home from work to pick up a loaf of bread without a big confrontation when they get home. If the jealousy is that bad, I advise Christian counseling.

For normal jealousy focused against you there are two important issues that must be faced. The first is, in order to build trust (the opposite to jealousy) we must never allow anything that would even suggest or appear to be the formation of flirting or a triangle situation. If anyone seems to be inching just a bit too close, put on the freeze. Pastors' wives have to guard against this, too. Anyone who is visible as church leaders is vulnerable and must constantly be on guard.

I normally sit on the front seat at church. But when I notice a man alone beginning to choose that location I change my seating. People will ask, "Why aren't you sitting up front these days?" I don't breathe it to a soul but when the situation changes (and it usually does), then I go back to wherever I feel is best.

Whenever a man calls about his personal problems during the hours my husband would not normally be home I immediately get on my guard. I might listen to his problem once, but at the close of that conversation I refer him to one of the other pastors.

Another issue is men coming to me for prayer. I don't make a big deal of it but I try to guide one of the other men over to pray with him.

When we were missionaries in Japan, a man who had come to Jesus through my ministry showed up at our front door asking me to pray with him. I knew he had walked two miles from the train station and it was awkward to turn him away. My husband was out of town and though our children were there, I didn't feel free to invite him in. Here was a new Christian who yearned to pray. What should I do?

In our front entry, we had two benches where people took off their shoes (a custom in Japan). I asked him to sit there a moment, put on my shoes, and ran down the hill to the Bible School, asking for one of the young ministry trainees to come and help. When we came back up the hill I told the new convert, "It isn't best to pray alone with the opposite sex so I have brought some help." I felt it was timely to teach both of them this important principle.

I was guarding not only my testimony, but was carefully making no room for jealousy to arise in our marriage relationship. Sometimes women want their husbands to think other men are looking at them and even make little remarks about it, but then they get upset when their husbands become jealous. Women are wise not to make those kind of remarks and, ladies, if you want no part of jealousy in your marriage don't make your husband jealous by what you say.

A *WOW* marriage gives space to both partners without fear or jealousy. And the ability to give each other proper space comes with trust. If that trust is ever broken it becomes difficult to give space.

The next two chapters cover vital principles related to the breaking of that trust. There is nothing apart from our relationship with Jesus, which is life itself, that is as sacred as the Christian marriage. All married couples should do everything possible to constantly build trust together, give each other plenty of space, and help each other enjoy their space freely. The tenth principle is give each other space.

Case in Point

Donald and Nancy were obviously angry when they entered my office. Nancy reminded me of a bird with a broken wing, and Donald was like a bull chasing a lamb. They were both Christians and their teenage children were serving the Lord, but they were angry and hard in spirit.

Donald wanted to do most of the talking, and she sat there sullen. He went on and on about how she didn't do anything to please him. She was rebellious and selfish and he couldn't stand her. It was awful how he talked about her. I wondered how much of this I should listen to. While he went on and on, she sat there silent, not saying a word. Finally I stopped him, and asked her if she had anything to say. Then the tears and the words poured out like a gusher. "No matter what I wear, he makes me change," she said. "He wants me to look sexy even around the house. Even on my day off, he insists that I wear make-up and wear the clothes he chooses. And he never leaves me alone—not even in the bathroom. He is always there, breathing down my back and I'm in prison."

As our sessions continued, I learned that he beat her when she resisted his demands. More than once she had to call the police, and she had often spent the night in the Battered Women's Shelter.

"Do you want this marriage to work?" I asked him one day. We had been dealing with the surface problems, but I knew it was time to begin striking at the root of their difficulties, which I believed was the need to give each other space.

Usually there is one of two reasons couples are afraid to give each other space: The desire to control their partner or jealousy and insecurity.

Sometimes it is both, which I felt was the case with this couple. When Donald vehemently showed me that he wanted this marriage to work, we began to deal with practical ways he was to begin giving Nancy space.

He was to let her choose her own wardrobe each day; never insist on her wearing make-up if she didn't want to; give her time alone, both at home and between her job and coming home in the evenings; deal with his demands of her in an unselfish way, and begin treating her with honor and respect, just as he would the Lord Jesus.

I would like to say that Donald worked beautifully with me and everything turned up roses, but it wasn't that easy. Before we completed very many counseling sessions, he would get angry at me and stomp out. He accused me of taking sides because I insisted he give Nancy space. And yet, he kept bouncing back and pleading for forgiveness, promising to do better.

He continued to insist that he wanted his marriage repaired. I worked with them for over a year. We had many stormy sessions where they would yell at each other or she would sob and scream. Oh, it was awful at times. But gradually, I saw the grace of God begin to work in both of them. It took much more than just the principle of their need to give each other space, but that was their main need. And as the months went by and they continued to come regularly to church and to counseling, God brought wonderful changes in their lives.

Today they are still together and are serving the Lord, and their children have made good marriages and are serving God. As I watched God's grace develop in their lives, I was made aware afresh how important it is to not only forgive the past, but also to let go of the present and give each other space. God has given us our yesterdays and our tomorrows, but it is today that He has given us as "the present" (gift) and it is in the present that we need to give each other space.

11

Be Accountable To Each Other

And Adam said, this is now bone of my bones, and flesh of my flesh . . . Therefore shall a man leave his father and his mother, and cleave unto his wife; and they shall be one flesh.

(Genesis 2:23-24)

When God presented Eve to Adam, He said, *"This is now bone of my bones, and flesh of my flesh . . . because she was taken out of man."* God did a beautiful thing in creating woman. He did not take her out of one of Adam's foot bones to be trampled on, nor one of his hand bones to be pushed around, but God took her from one of Adam's ribs right next to his heart, to be loved, protected, and provided for. Marriage, as many things in life, comes in three dimensions: leaving, cleaving, and weaving. We must leave our life of singleness. We must leave our life of dependence on our family. We must leave our former life of independence and thinking only of ourselves.

Now, someone else shares us in a new and vital way: shares everything we have, everything we are, and everything we will ever become. Every moment now we are accountable to each other. This is part of leaving the past and cleaving to each other and weaving our lives together. Because of this a man must leave his father and mother, cleave to his wife and weave their lives together into a new family and a new home. *"And they shall be one flesh."* This adjustment is not always easy. Some couples have problems because one partner doesn't really leave father and mother.

This is where in-law problems come in. Sometimes without intending to, one may continue to lean too much on parents, instead of cleaving to the spouse and weaving their lives together into a new family.

The longer couples go without children, the more difficult this can be. Children make you dependent on each other. Children force you to cleave to each other and weave your lives around them.

Sure, there will be times when you will seek the wise counsel of your parents, but all first place intimacy must go to your spouse. And never under any condition, should your little tiffs or criticisms of your spouse be shared with your family or in-laws. There must be complete leaving and total cleaving to each other.

When you were a child your parents gave you permission to go places and they usually knew where you were and with whom. Now that you are married that place belongs to your partner. Not that you must obtain permission like a child but there should always be an understanding, an accountability to each other.

In our work we go in and out of our house frequently. Usually we know each other's schedule beforehand but there are times when one of us will come and go and we miss each other all day. To keep our commitment to accountability we leave a note on the kitchen table. This way we always know where the other one is and with whom and it helps to build trust. Some days there are several notes. This is important and couples who fail to do this are missing out in cleaving and weaving their lives together.

Another important principle is that regardless of the circumstance, neither of us is ever excluded from the other's life. If we're counseling separately, eating lunch with someone or are on the phone, whatever our activity might be, the other knows that always, they are welcome to participate.

I never feel restricted from my husband's office, no matter with whom he is meeting or whatever is going on. I am his wife, and therefore, I always belong. We are one flesh. He knows he always belongs wherever I might be or with whomever. Whether in counseling, in praying or in visiting, he is always a welcome part of my life. We are one flesh.

Because of this, if one of us has the flu or something, we automatically feel it is wise to sleep separately. Usually the one who is not sick sleeps in another room. This is done without strain or insecure feelings. We both know it is in the best interest of the one who is down plus it might keep the well person from infection.

Not only are we to be answerable to each other at all times as one flesh, we must also be open and honest. Not in a cruel way. No cutdowns are allowed if this is to be a *WOW* marriage. When someone says to me, "Please don't tell a living soul" I always warn them ahead of time. "I have no secrets from my husband. Anything you tell me, you must be willing for me to share it with him." He treats me the same way, though we are careful to never betray anyone's confidence.

Marriage is wonderful when as one flesh we can feel the other's feelings, and share our deepest emotions. When two hearts as one unite, the yoke is easy and the burden is light. When you are one flesh and one is hurt, the other can taste the salt from their tears.

I can remember how my beautiful mother was a sympathetic listener anytime one of us got bruised or had a tummy ache or the slightest ache or pain. She was there for us and always expressed her care and concern. It made us want to share with her every feeling we had. This was good, for this sharing continued through our difficult teen years and she was still there to hear and care. She also gave us valuable guidance and I treasure those memories.

But in leaving her I found that I could cleave to a most wonderful, understanding man who also cares about the deepest feelings or hurts that might come. This is the *WOW* marriage where we weave our lives together after we have left the past and cleaved to each other. This sharing of our deepest thoughts and needs without fear of scorn or ridicule comes only if both are constantly answerable to each other.

Neither spouse should ever answer a question on where one has been or with whom, with the retort, "Why do you want to know?" That kind of an answer destroys trust.

It should be a given between you that each of you is accountable to the other at all times, whether you are together or whether you are apart. Accountability helps to build trust in the relationship. It's the basis of discipleship and without it all of us are vulnerable.

In the tragedy of couples who have been broken by an affair, it can almost always be traced to the fact that there was not the proper accountability in their relationship. While we are to completely trust each other, a word of caution is in order here. Don't be naive. Be alert to signs of danger or temptation. Without being jealous or picky, every spouse should be on constant guard to protect the purity of the marriage. There's a difference between being jealous and being wise and alert. A lot of problems can be averted by godly wisdom in this area.

If there should be a problem of infidelity the guilty person must go overboard to restore that trust so needed in a good marriage. Forgiveness is usually possible and will be discussed in the next chapter, but rebuilding trust is not as easy as building trust in the first place, and adding to that trust as the years go by. This is why being true to your original trust and your marriage vows is very vital.

Memories have a dreadful way of bringing back hurts and wounds, and though a spouse may forgive (and must), the fear of a repeated failure is difficult to overcome. But it's worth trying. God is able to restore completely and forgiveness brings beautiful healing.

Couples should talk about the issue of accountability without any sense of distrust. You should both have an understanding of what areas you need to be alert to; where boundaries are; know the pitfalls and how to avoid them, and constantly make new vocal declarations to each other of your commitment and love.

Every now and then couples should tell each other they are renewing their 100% commitment to love, cherish and obey until death do us part. Don't be like the man who said he told his wife he loved her before they got married, and if he changed his mind he would let her know. That isn't enough. We should declare our love and fidelity to each other frequently. This helps to bring security and trust. Your verbal confession brings tremendous dynamics into a good marriage.

It has been well said that everyone needs a friend, a mentor, and a disciple. As married people, we become a mentor to each other in a sense, though it is more horizontal than vertical. In marriage, we are all three: we are best of friends, we are mentors, and also disciples. This is accountability. We must be answerable to each other in all areas, fulfilling principle number eleven in the *WOW* Christian marriage.

Number eleven in our twelve principles for a *WOW* marriage is the importance of being accountable. Be accountable to each other at all times. Remember, you are one flesh, and the eleventh principle of accountability is important to your *WOW* marriage!

Case in Point

Randy and Rita had already filed for divorce. They had five beautiful children in our Christian school and we just couldn't let this happen. Randy was a truck driver and she a school teacher. For years they had gone their own ways with the policy between them of "Live and let live." But Rita had a shopping obsession and every time a new credit card application came in the mail, she would fill it out and send it in. Then she would go to the malls and max it out.

Randy was so in debt, he didn't know which way to turn. He made good money on his job but it couldn't begin to keep up with Rita's spending drive. He enjoyed driving, and more and more he dreaded going home because of the bill collectors, and Rita's constant new purchases. It was easier to stay away.

Along his routes Randy had developed several women friends. After all, there was no way Rita could ever find out, and he needed some enjoyment in life. He wasn't accountable to anyone so it really didn't matter. Once in awhile he thought about God, and how he and his kids really needed Him, but as long as they could keep the children in the Christian school, hopefully they would be okay.

With Randy gone so much, Rita too had made some close friends among the male teachers at the school where she taught. Several of them were divorced and it was easy to get together for lunch or dinner in the evenings after she had touched base with the kids. No one would ever know, and as long as the kids were in a good environment, surely everything was fine.

But sin is progressive, and Satan's snares are never as innocent as he would have you to believe. Randy and Rita were at the bottom of the barrel in every area of their relationship. When we heard they had filed for divorce, I had to run them down. Randy was out of town most of the time, and when he was in town, he was usually catching up on sleep in order to go out again. It was difficult, but we persisted.

When they finally came for counseling, they were like two strangers, and their faces were gloomy and dark. Condemnation and guilt were written all over them and they looked the picture of hopelessness. I knew nothing of their financial problems or their immorality. All I saw was misery and guilt. To make it worse, neither of them wanted the marriage. They didn't like each other and called each other names. He said she was a fat slob and she said he was a no good lazy bum.

While they continued this spouse bashing, all I could see was five beautiful children whose lives were about to be wrecked because of the lack of accountability in the lives of their parents.

As I often do when I'm not sure where to start, I opened up to 1 Corinthians 7:3 *"Let the husband render unto the wife due benevolence; and likewise also the wife unto the husband."*

Most couples don't have the foggiest idea what "due benevolence" means, so we worked on that for a few minutes. As Christians, God requires us to give ourselves to each other without expecting anything in return, and to give and give and keep giving. I didn't mention their filing for divorce, but was groping my way, silently asking the Holy Spirit for help each step.

Suddenly Rita began to weep, and Randy looked startled. She spilled it all out—all about her affairs, how bitter she had been at Randy, how she knew the reason he didn't come home was because he had other women. It went on and on, and Randy then began to melt. He knew he had been doing wrong; he had shirked his responsibility as a father, but he had felt trapped. What was he supposed to do, when no sooner did he pay off one credit card than she maxed out another?

And thus began some long months of counseling built on the principle of accountability. It took several sessions before they both repented for their unfaithfulness, and many more before they were able to forgive each other. As God worked in their hearts, each session became a time of building their character with teaching. I gave them 1 Peter 3:7:

> *Likewise, ye husbands, dwell with them according to knowledge, giving honor unto the wife, as unto the weaker vessel, and as being heirs together of the grace of life; that your prayers be not hindered.*

I drove home the concept of how God desires they leave (their past), cleave, and weave their lives together and that they must not only be accountable at all times to each other, but also, when separated geographically, they must each be accountable to another Christian.

It has been six years now since the divorce was canceled. Rita still has someone in the church to whom she regularly is accountable, besides their constant communication by phone to each other when he is away, and Randy has found another Christian driver that he meets routinely on his runs to whom he is accountable. Through the teaching on accountability, Rita has stopped signing up new credit cards and at this writing, their bills are nearly paid up, and she has agreed to only buy on the credit with his permission. More than ever, through the tragedy of their immorality and the suffering it brought, they are aware of being bone of each other's bones and one flesh, always accountable to each other and always accountable to God and their five children.

12

Forgive!

*Be ye kind one to another, tenderhearted, forgiving
one another, even as God for Christ's sake hath forgiven
you.*

(Ephesians 4:32)

Scripture commands us to be kind, tenderhearted, and forgiving. This is easy toward someone living on the other side of the globe, but difficult when you are close and the offense is frequent. Though I don't know where they originated, I once heard a minister quote these words:

> To live above with those we love
> Oh, that will be glory!
> To live below with those we know
> Now that's another story.

It will help if we can understand the words, *"for Christ's sake."* That's what God did, He forgave us for Christ's sake; because Jesus gave His all that we might be forgiven. And now God sees us as if we had never sinned. He has erased our past and never remembers it against us again.

In the marriage relationship an apology and verbalized forgiveness work wonders. In fifty-plus years of our *WOW* marriage, there hasn't been a whole lot that needed forgiveness.

As already mentioned, one of my most difficult hang-ups has been to fix a lovely meal and wait and wait with no husband showing up. Finally, hours later, when he does come home, I have become sullen. My spirit gets hard, I don't want to communicate and it's like I'm in a vice from which I can't get free. I have tried singing praises aloud to God at this point, and still the problem continues in my offended spirit.

In Ephesians 4:32, Paul said that we are not only to be kind and forgiving, we are also to be tenderhearted. The moment we allow our spirit to get hard, we are no longer kind and tenderhearted. This hardness springs from a wrong decision based on selfishness. From years of experience, I know now that the only reason Johnny is late is because of an emergency, or he forgot to tell me about a luncheon engagement, or something similar. I thank God that this is not a big problem though it is something I am still working on in me.

What amazes me is that I can be irritated at him for being late but the moment he apologizes it instantly melts away. What a wonderful miracle forgiveness brings. It is a marvellous tool that God has given us for building strong relationships.

When I struggle with this I ask myself over and over, why I don't redeem the situation ahead of time and forgive even before he apologizes. This is what I'm working on now. In chapter two where we dealt with the contest of unselfishness, we used the Scripture in Luke 6:38, *"Give and it shall be given unto you."* This is a favorite verse with many. However, the verse just above it, verse 37, says, *"Forgive, and ye shall be forgiven."* This infers that if we don't forgive, then God won't forgive us.

Jesus built on this concept in Matthew 18 when he told the parable of the servant who owed the king ten thousand talents (equivalent to ten million dollars), who was forgiven and released from his huge debt.

But the servant went out and found another man who owed him an hundred pence (equivalent to $20), and though the fellow servant fell down at his feet and begged for mercy, he threw him into prison until he could pay the whole amount. When the king heard it, he became angry and turned his servant over to the tormentors. In verse 35, Jesus said: *"Likewise shall my heavenly Father do also unto you, if ye from your hearts forgive not every one his brother their trespasses."*

Who today would be the "tormentors?" When we coddle unforgiveness it brings tormenting memories and bitterness, and opens the door for satanic powers to build strongholds in our personalities. I never want to be turned over to the tormentors. It is much better to forgive. Paul, while admonishing us to forgive, says that unforgiveness gives Satan an advantage over us (2 Corinthians 2: 10,11).

Unforgiveness imprisons you in your past, makes you miserable in the present, and shrinks your potential in the future. It paralyzes your creativity, shrinks your initiative, and destroys your self confidence. It also blocks out your relationship with God and hinders your faith, bringing you under a dark blanket of hardness and condemnation. Forgiveness doesn't cheapen you (contrary to the devil's lies), it enhances your dignity, and makes you more like God. It makes you transparent. Forgiveness sets you free from the past and speeds the healing process of the hurts.

Years ago we had been wounded by criticism from someone we loved dearly. One day, sitting in the municipal auditorium here in San Antonio, we heard a message on forgiveness, and for the first time were quickened with the understanding that forgiveness is not a feeling, nor the result of a feeling—it is a simple choice. It's a decision that you make deliberately, whether there is an apology or not.

I wept as I opened my spirit to this teaching, for the wound had continued several years. We had tried confrontation to no avail, and had asked others to help but nothing seemed to work. That day, sitting in the auditorium, we made the choice to forgive regardless. This set us free, and the wound began to heal.

The criticism didn't stop, but it was almost fun to be able to tell those who came with the gossip, "You tell them that we have decided to forgive." We said this every time someone came to us with some negative talk about the situation. Before long the criticism stopped and the walls came down.

Forgiveness is a miracle of the heart, and it bridges the gaps that have been made in our relationships through strenuous circumstances. No wonder Jesus taught the disciples in His model prayer to pray, "Forgive us our trespasses, as we forgive those who trespass against us." Forgive because God has commanded it.

In Mark 11:26, Jesus said that if we do not forgive each other neither will our Father which is in heaven forgive us. Another strong admonition is in Mark 11:25: *"And when ye stand praying, forgive, if ye have aught against any; that your Father also which is in heaven may forgive you your trespasses.*" To forgive is to let go and rise above the offense. It is letting go to the extent that like God, we refuse to ever remember it again.

How many times do we stand in church to pray and have unforgiveness in our hearts? This must never be. God said that when we stand to pray we must forgive. My prayer is that God will teach me to forgive instantly and totally the moment an offense arises, to the extent that I never think of it again, much less ever mention it to a soul. This is important in a *WOW* marriage.

In Psalms 119:165, David said that if we love God's law we will have great peace and *"nothing shall offend."* More than once, Johnny has quoted this verse to me when I have let my feelings get hurt. He knows I love God's Word, and thus if I allow my heart to be wounded I am contradicting the Scripture. Do we really love God's law? If so, we must forgive, let go and forget.

Some people have a dreadful time bringing their minds into the concept of forgiveness. Their wounds have been of severe proportions and repeatedly deepened until their emotions feel frayed and broken. When they call for a counseling appointment they usually add the phrase "And I just cannot forgive."

Women who have been abused repeatedly and been taken advantage of have a hard time with this. Like Peter they want to ask "How many more times do I forgive?" One couple who had been separated over two years because of his three affairs came for counseling. They were religious people, though obviously unsaved. She was reluctant to come, but came only to please him. She felt there was no hope for him, and certainly there was no hope for their marriage. How could she ever trust him again?

We counseled together each week for ten months. They were still separated, and she had no intention of moving back in with him. But the Word of God began to work in their hearts. And everything began to change. They kept coming, though they didn't attend our church. As they began to grasp the concept of forgiveness, not only with each other, but also from the Lord, it was easy to lead them to Jesus. What a beautiful day it was when they knelt together asking God to forgive them for their broken vows and for their unforgiveness toward each other. In helping to lead couples into repentance and forgiveness, I insist that they verbalize the words to each other, "I do forgive you." This helps to seal up their acceptance of the apology. We do this, and then have each of them repent out loud to the Lord. The exciting part that I see over and over is, when we get up off our knees, repentance brings the estranged couple right into each other's arms.

"I am ready to go back and try again. God has done a miracle of forgiveness in my heart. I will endeavor to trust again" said the wife who had been deceived three times and had vowed she would never go back to him.

That was fifteen years ago and today they are a beautiful family, serving the Lord with joy. It can happen to anyone. It can happen to you. Some situations take time, but don't give up. The battle is worth it, especially where there are children.

Refuse to receive accusations and hurts that you know do not belong to you. Remember that Satan is the accuser and he often initiates false accusations to bring paralysis. A lady once told me that I was a manipulator, and I said as sweetly as I could, "It would be kinder to say I motivate." But that stung in my spirit for a long time, and I allowed the devil to use it to paralyze me at times when I knew the Lord wanted me to step out and help someone. If instead, I had instantly forgiven and let go of the accusation, it would have had no effect on me at all.

As workers in God's kingdom we need to be alert to false accusations and renounce them when they come. We need to see that these accusations are nothing but a smoke screen from Satan to paralyze our ministry and make us ineffective for God. Sometimes they are given by someone who is possibly jealous of our ministry.

We are foolish to succumb to accusations that we know are not true. John said, in Revelation 12:10, that Satan is the accuser. In our marriage we must be very careful about this area of accusing each other. Anytime we say "You always . . ." or "You never . . . ," it is demeaning to the other's character, and gives Satan an advantage. Instead, when our spouse does something that wounds us, we should address the behavior, and not accuse the character. Character is the person himself, and when it is attacked it is hard to forget.

In the above situation, when I asked the person who wounded me what I had done to offend, the answer I received was, "It's not anything you've done, it's just YOU." What could I do? I couldn't become "un-me." Even in such unexplainable, complex situations, the bottom line is instant forgiveness. When I forgave and spoke my forgiveness aloud over and over, healing and restoration came.

More recently someone came to me upset because I had to correct a teenager in our church, dealing with it as wisely and tenderly as I knew how. The person who came to me was not related to the teen nor involved in any way. But with heated anger he started pouring on false accusations.

I was so thankful the Lord reminded me to apologize, even though I felt I had obeyed the Lord in dealing with the case. Should we apologize even when we are right? I believe we should. Not only for their sakes, but for our own. My apology was an acknowledgment that as a human, I could have made a mistake. We are not infallible. But what my apology did for me was, it dismissed all the mean things he had said. It made him feel better, and helped me to shake it all off.

Jesus said that it was inevitable but that offenses will come in life. Then, how many times are we to forgive the same person? Peter had a problem with this question, and in Matthew 18:21, he asked Jesus if seven times a day wasn't enough? We know Jesus' tremendous answer: *"I say not unto thee until seven times, but seventy times seven."* Wow! I have never had to forgive anyone seven times, much less seventy times seven.

Corrie Ten Boon, who was desperately mistreated because she helped rescue Jews from the Germans during World War II, tells how she had a battle over forgiving the man who raped her sister and was finally responsible for her death. She was traveling in America, sharing her testimony and speaking on forgiveness, when at the close of the service one night he showed up at the front wanting to shake her hand and receive forgiveness.

He had become a Christian. Prior to this she had thought she had dealt with her own unforgiveness toward him and that it was all over. But that night when he showed up and reached out his hand toward her, she froze in her spirit, and could not bring her hand out to shake his. Later that night at her hotel room, she wept before the Lord, begging Him to help her forgive this man. How could she go on teaching others about forgiveness unless she herself was able to forgive? That night God spoke peace to her heart. He told her that yes, she had forgiven the man; that she had chosen to forgive, though it was very hard; but that sometimes the feelings of forgiveness take time to develop.

The Lord reminded her of the old church bell that is rung by pulling a rope. Even after a person stops pulling the rope, the bell keeps ringing, but gradually, the rings get shorter and shorter, and finally stop altogether. God told her that her feelings of unforgiveness would eventually stop, just as the church bell does. Later I heard her testify that the feelings had completely stopped. This was based on her quality decision: her decision to forgive.

A man called me one day, sobbing. His wife had moved in with a real young man, and he was devastated. Through the months he'd call now and then and ask me to pray with his two children, who were also devastated. They were around seven and nine years old. Several times I took them aside and we prayed together for restoration of the marriage, and for forgiveness in each heart. Then one day, the father called again. "What shall I do? My wife is pregnant by this other man and he has now deserted her, and she wants to come home and wants me to receive the baby as mine."

This was a big order for him. How could he ever forgive her? How could he love this little baby that belonged to another man? He was afraid he would resent it; that it would always be a reminder of those terrible months when she had abandoned her family. Up until this point, she had been hard and unreachable, but now, she needed his help and support.

They came for counseling together, and it was exciting how God moved in both of them. She surrendered her life to the Lord, and after some deep dealings of God, he was able to completely forgive. The marriage was restored, and today the family is simply beautiful. People on the outside know nothing about their past, and the child has fit in just like she was theirs. What a wonderful testimony this has been to the older children. God answered their prayers.

What a tragic ending this true account could have had. What if the husband had refused to forgive? He would have become bitter, and his bitterness would have spread to all of the family. Hebrews 12:15 warns us about bitterness: *"Looking diligently lest any man fail of the grace of*

God; lest any root of bitterness springing up trouble you, and thereby many be defiled." Bitterness, Scripture says, is like a root that spreads. Everywhere it goes, it brings trouble and defilement. But the grace of God enables us to forgive, even in the hardest circumstance.

Once, when I was battling with unforgiveness, God quickened Zechariah 4:7 to me: *"Who art thou, O great mountain? before Zerubbabel thou shalt become a plain: and he shall bring forth the headstone thereof with shoutings, crying Grace, grace unto it."*

The Lord showed me that I should shout "Grace, grace" toward the person who had wounded me. As I did this each morning in my prayer time, it was like a miracle. I rose completely above it. And I actually enjoyed praying for God's grace to abound in the person I'd had a problem with.

Like the song goes, "God's grace is marvellous beyond our understanding." So if you are having a hard time forgiving, apply God's grace to your situation. Shout "Grace, grace" to your mountain, and you too will be able to rise above it. God has promised that the mountain will become a plain. And it will. And remember, Jesus is the "headstone."

Every day then, in your *WOW* marriage, make sure that your heart is open and transparent—no hidden agendas, no bitterness, no bad memories or hurts that you have failed to forgive. Forgive and forget them.

Forgive them and shake them off, just like the Apostle Paul shook off the poisonous serpent that came out of the fire and wrapped around his wrist on the isle of Mileta. Was it not enough that Paul was a prisoner on his way to Rome, had been shipwrecked, swam to this island in the pouring rain and cold, and now was in danger of dying by snakebite? He didn't question God and get bitter. Instead he shook it off. And you can also shake off your offenses.

Whatever happens in your life, determine to forgive and forget—shake it off. Remember, just as the poisonous viper could not harm Paul because he shook it off, those things that have come against you cannot hurt you if you will shake them off in forgiveness.

This is a new day, and God makes all things new as we trust Him and walk in His ways. So number twelve in our *WOW* marriage is forgive, let go, and forget.

Case in Point

"Are you Mrs. Smith?" the young woman at the door asked. "I am Gerry Watson, and this is my baby by your husband, and I've come to demand child support. And in case you don't believe me, look at this" and she held up a large photograph of herself, her baby, and Jimmy with his arms around them. Betty felt like she was going to faint. There was the evidence right in front of her. And Jimmy had always wanted a son. Not that he didn't love their three little girls, but every man has that inborn strong desire to have a son.

Why would God give him a son through another woman? She fought back the tears and hardly heard Gerry's outpouring of demands for money.

"And if you don't get some child support to me immediately, I am going to the District Attorney's office and Jimmy will be arrested. Good-bye."

When they came for counseling, Jimmy and Betty came in two cars. She had already insisted that he move out. As he glued his eyes to the floor, I was reminded of the Scripture in Proverbs 6:32,33 where it speaks about the adulterous man: "*A wound and dishonor shall he get and his reproach shall not be wiped away.*"

Betty loved Jimmy and really didn't want a divorce, but at that point, she was hurt and bitter and felt there was no other way to go. When we read Scriptures on forgiveness,

I felt it hit a brick wall. She sat there numb, while he sat and wept over his sins. Each time they came, I had to be exceedingly gentle and tender, for they were both delicate, sensitive personalities.

At times Jimmy was suicidal, and this frightened Betty. She would call in the middle of the night when she had received a call from him. She didn't know which way to turn. She was confused and disoriented. Fortunately, her parents were both strong Christians, and they loved Jimmy, and kept urging her to forgive him and pick up her life again. But they lived in another state so I suggested she take a leave of absence and go visit them for awhile.

When Betty returned from her visit, I sensed that we had reached the peak of the problem. She wasn't quite ready to forgive yet, but she asked me to give her a list of verses on forgiveness. How grateful I was for the power of God's Word. Here were two broken lives, wounded by Satan and sin—confused, condemned. How could they once again be free and happy?

Forgiveness cannot be pushed on someone else prematurely. I knew I had to wait for God's Spirit to ripen the fruit. That if I pulled the petals from the rose bud too soon, I could make the whole thing abort. It was a delicate time. So I waited. We continued to memorize Scriptures on forgiveness each week. We emphasized the power of Christ's blood to totally forgive and erase the past. Over and over we dealt with letting go, just like Paul shook off the snake that grabbed his arm at the camp fire on the island of Miletas, after he was shipwrecked.

I told them the story of Joseph who was sold by his own brothers, and framed by Mrs. Potiphar when he was true to God, then thrown into the dungeon and forgotten by the two men whom he befriended and whose dreams he interpreted. On the day that his first son was born, he declared that he was to be named Manasseh, which means *forgetting.* That's how completely he forgave all those who had wronged him for the previous twenty-one years. He named his next son, Ephraim, which means *fruitful.* Instead of being all dried up with bitterness, he forgot the past, picked up his life and moved forward with tremendous blessings from God and was fruitful in the land. Even to the point of not only saving all of Egypt, but his own family and his brothers as well.

Gradually I saw the hardness in Betty begin to melt. What a beautiful day it was when she finally turned to her husband and said through tears, "Jimmy, I've decided to completely forgive you. I'm not sure how long it will take for me to ever trust you again, but right now, I am determined to forgive you. I don't want to coddle bitterness, and I don't want to bring it up anymore. Can you forgive me for all the mean things I have said to you?"

With that, we three got on our knees and poured it all out to the Lord. As Jimmy had done many times before, he again asked God to forgive him, and help him be a good husband and father. As he again asked Betty to forgive him, she opened her arms and they became one. It was a beautiful scene. Jimmy moved back home. The children were delighted.

Because Gerry would not leave the family alone, Jimmy and Betty moved away. But the delightsome part is, God gave them another child—a little son. They named him Jimmy.

Recently (several years after the events related here), they came back to thank us for helping establish their truly *WOW* Christian marriage.

13

Tying It All Together

Christ's Lordship, the unselfishness contest, joyfully serving, refusing strife and criticism, never compare, don't threaten, never say no, humor, honor and respect, giving space, accountability, and forgiveness—these are all integral parts of a truly *WOW* marriage. All of these are important, and just like with the human body, if one is absent, problems arise.

Nearly five years ago, I had a mastectomy. Instead of going through chemotherapy or radiation, I began taking large amounts of vitamins, minerals, and herbs. Though I am nearly five years older than before the cancer struck, I am much healthier and have more energy. I believe this is because the program I'm on is quickening every area of my physical being.

So it is in a marriage. Though during counseling it may be evident that in one area the greatest need seems to surface, allowing us a point at which to begin, all twelve principles of a *WOW* marriage must ultimately be adopted and applied in order to work.

Those who do pastoral counseling would be wise to memorize these twelve principles and get into the habit of watching for their absence as couples begin to share their problems. The Bible always has an answer for every situation, and if we go into the counseling sessions with that confidence, we need never feel nervous about the outcome, no matter how difficult the situation.

When I began counseling, I felt apprehensive about the unknown. What if I didn't know which way to go? What if I couldn't think of a Scripture to meet their need? At first, I kept several outlines with connected Scriptures in my top desk drawer just in case I drew a blank. But all that was superfluous, as the Holy Spirit always came to my rescue and showed me which direction to take. That way, when God gave us success, all the glory went back to Him.

God gave us many successes, but not in every case. More than once I've had unsaved husbands jump up and stomp out the door when I've tried to bring them to a decision to receive Christ as Savior. An atheist did this once and I felt really bad, thinking I had blown it. But months later his wife called to say that day was a turning point in their marriage, and her husband had been saved in a Baptist church where they were now attending.

When I was working on my degree in counseling, my professors urged me to go after a state license. "You can then hang up your shingle and make $100 an hour!" they challenged. But I wasn't interested in that. To me, pastoral counseling is meeting people's needs where they are. It is bringing healing and restoration. It is saving couples and children from terrible hurts and bitterness that can scar them for life. It is leading people on a one-to-one basis to the foot of the Cross of Jesus, and seeing repentance and forgiveness.

One thing I have learned in this modern age of free sex and common immorality: many couples live under horrible guilt and condemnation because they had sex before they were married. This brings a sense of abuse into their subconsciousness. Even Christians fall prey to this. The man violates the woman and goes on for years in the shadow of that condemnation. She violates him by not being strong enough to resist which brings her under guilt and condemnation.

One of the last questions I ask couples when we get on our knees at the end of a session is if they had sex before they were married. These days, it is a rare couple who has not. Very few girls nowadays are virgins when they approach the altar. There, on our knees, I have them bare their hearts to each other, apologizing for violating the other's body, even years before. This brings a release, and many couples have told me what a relief it has been to them to be thus freed from the burden of guilt they have borne so long.

In Psalm 73:24, David says God will guide us with His counsel, and in Psalm 1:1, we are told that the person who refuses the counsel of the ungodly is blessed. In Proverbs 11:14, the wise man said, "*Where no counsel is, the people fall.*" And we have seen the tragedy of this over and over as families break up and children are torn apart, all because there was no one close by who could give them godly counsel and help.

Proverbs 12:15 says, *"The way of a fool is right in his own eyes, but he that hearkeneth unto counsel is wise."* Proverbs 15:22 says, *"Without counsel purposes are disappointed, but in the multitude of counselors they are established."*

Should you receive counseling? Anytime your marriage isn't what God wants, you need help. But be careful to go only to those who will give you biblical counsel, and be sure they will keep your situation totally confidential.

There is no problem too hard for God, and as I bring this chapter to an end, I do so with the prayer that you who read this will not only apply all twelve of these biblical principles to your marriage, you will also allow God to use you to help others to walk in these principles. In doing so, their marriages can also become *WOW!*

14

Hang In There

An Appendage

She sat staring into space. The house was so silent.
What had she done? Oh, if she could only turn back the
clock! Billows of sobs engulfed her again and again. What
was there to live for now? The children—yes yes, I must
pick myself up and be strong for them. But how? How can
I raise them alone? How can my little son ever understand
his manhood without his daddy?

And as they grow older, will they begin to blame me
for the breakup of our marriage? What shall I tell them?
Do I tell them their dad is a hopeless drunk who lived with

one woman after another? Do I tell them that for twelve years I have forgiven him again and again and taken him back? Do I tell them the truth and embitter them with my pain, or do I teach them respect for their father by whom they have been rejected and hurt?

"Oh God! Show me what to do" she sobbed out loud. "Life is too difficult, the road is too long and the obstacles are too many. How can I lead my three children without their father's help? Lord, you invented marriage and family, and you intended there be two parents, not just one. How can I go on alone?" The tears began to pour like a river. She decided to go and check his closet. Had he come over while she was at work and gotten his things?

His closet was empty. Totally empty—even his shoes were gone. Why did his shoes mean that much to her? She couldn't understand her feelings—it was just that they had been together. Oh, how she loved him—in spite of his faults—in spite of his drinking and other women.

She could never forget his strong arms and his beautiful smile. He was generous, he was fun to be with, and always patient and understanding with her and the kids. Now he would be in someone else's arms. How would the kids feel about the other woman?

"Why didn't I receive his apology and take him back as I'd done so many times before? God! Are you there anywhere?" she wailed, staring at the empty closet. "Can you restore us somehow? Can you forgive me for filing for divorce in my anger and hurt? Your Word says that nothing is impossible with you. God is there any hope left for Tony and me?"

Tina had expected the pain to lesson after she filed. She had been confused and hurt for so long, all she wanted to do was put closure to her marriage and get on with her life. But she didn't expect her emotions to react the way they were. Guilt and embarrassment overwhelmed her constantly. She began to avoid people—even her friends. She felt alone, ashamed, defeated.

Why? Why? was her constant question. Everywhere she turned she felt trapped by her guilt and her pain. She sat alone at church—felt all alone, even at work. Her life began to take on a sense of darkness. She became irritated at her children—irritated at her mother and brothers who had stood graciously by her. Now, all she wanted to do was lash out at everyone, blame everyone and just be alone.

The house was too quiet. Did Tony take his tackle box? "I'd better go check" she mused. But the garage seemed just as empty as the house. The side where he normally parked his car seemed to scream out at her in accusation. Not only was all his fishing equipment gone, everything related to him was gone. His caps, his tools, his baseball glove—everything was gone!

It all seemed so empty, just like her empty heart. "If only I had tried harder! I know we could have made it together. Now I am all alone. Where do I go from here?"

Her whole world had crashed around her. If only she could hear his voice, feel his touch, smell his smell. But that was over. It had ended. The divorce had cut them apart—they were no longer one flesh. He wouldn't be coming home. All their vows had gone down the drain. She was no longer a "wife" but just one of millions of divorcees who had failed. She knew she had failed God. She had failed her husband, failed her children, and had failed herself.

Would life ever be normal again? Would she forever be haunted with this sense of failure and darkness?

Dear Reader,

Perhaps you think you have tried everything. Nothing seems to have worked, and you are ready to throw in the towel. If that's you, this chapter will hopefully help you to see the consequences of breaking those sacred vows.

What does the Bible say about divorce? And what do famous people like Bill Gothard say about it?

Something as serious as a divorce should never be entered into without serious consideration and prayer about all the issues involved. Too often, couples break up in a fit of anger or hurts, only to regret it later. Once you have become "one flesh" before the Lord, it is impossible to "unscramble the eggs." Your emotions are permanently connected and the fracture is much harder and more painful than you had thought it would be.

Throughout our ministry, we have often heard the words, "I can't wait to get on with my life. Anything would be better than the hell he's putting me through" only to hear the same person say years later, "I should have forgiven and stayed with my first marriage. I could have made it, if I'd tried harder. If only I had, I wouldn't be in the mess I am today."

There are nine major negatives that result from divorce which we will list here, then will comment on briefly:

When a Person Files for Divorce:

1. It is the result of hardness of heart:

> *He saith unto them, Moses because of the hardness*
> *of your hearts suffered you to put away your wives: but*
> *from the beginning it was not so.*
> (Matthew 19:8)

Remember how tender your heart was on your wedding night? Your spouse could do nothing wrong. You were both excited just to be together. Goose bumps and lovey-dovies were everywhere. When your hearts melt with forgiveness, that can all be restored. Hardness of heart is an awful thing; it is like a vise strangling you. It controls your thoughts day and night distracting you from progress in any area, killing your initiative and creativity. And the tragedy is, simple divorce doesn't actually put an end to it as you had hoped.

2. It increases exposure to Satan's strongholds:

> *And the Lord God said, It is not good that a man*
> *should be alone; I will make him an help meet for him.*
> (Genesis 2:18)

> *It is good for a man not to touch a woman.*
> *Nevertheless, to avoid fornication, let every man*
> *have his own wife, and let every woman have her own*
> *husband.*
> (1 Corinthians 7:1,2)

No matter how pure and moral you have always been, you are not immune. No one is. For you to think this is not a hazard for you is deception. With every divorce, the immorality in our culture tends to increase. God's Word declares it. God created marriage for the purpose of establishing godly homes and the development of a godly seed. Each of us makes an impact on our culture, and God has called us to be a nation of righteousness, not immorality. A divorced man or woman is vulnerable to immorality.

3. Blasphemes God's Word:

The aged women likewise . . .

That they may teach the young women to be sober, to love their husbands, to love their children,

To be discreet, chaste, keepers at home, good, obedient to their own husbands, that the word of God be not blasphemed.

(Titus 2:3-5)

As Christians, our whole lifestyle is based on the promises in God's Word. When we give up on our marriage, we are declaring failure to the world. Our confession is then that God's promises failed. He did not change our mate. We prayed and stood upon His Word, and it did not happen. This blasphemes God's Word. Instead, God has a pattern, a beautiful pattern for a happy Christian home that is based on the principles in the above verses. But our culture has thrown out those principles, and as a result, divorces and heartbreaks have multiplied and God's Word has been blasphemed.

4. The Christian's Witness is Weakened or Even Destroyed:

I know both how to be abased, and I know how to abound: everywhere and in all things . . . both to abound and to suffer need.

I can do all things through Christ which strengtheneth me.
(Philippians 4:12-13)

When one gives up and gets a divorce, his failure points back to his Christian testimony. Like our last point, all the witnessing of the past is neutralized. We can no longer say *"I can do all things through Christ,"* because something went wrong. Not only is God's Word blasphemed, our personal witness is rendered powerless. The world isn't looking for philosophies that don't work. They want reality lived out daily in the home and in the market place.

5. Destroys Many Families:

For none of us liveth to himself, and no man dieth to himself.
But why dost thou judge thy brother? or why dost thou set at nought thy brother? for we shall all stand before the judgment seat of Christ.
... but judge this rather, that no man put a stumbling block or an occasion to fall in his brother's way.
(Romans 14:7,10,13)

Divorce does dreadful things to families. Grandparents and children are torn apart. Hatred and strife become the thing of the day. Christmases and birthdays become difficult and all broken up. Every part of the family is wounded and fractured. Lies and accusations fly in the face of innocent family members. Bitterness leads to brokenness, and families who used to be friends are suddenly made into enemies. Disappointment and distrust prevail.

It is not only the divorcing couple who is affected, but all the cousins, aunts, uncles, and relatives on both sides are caught up in the quicksand of hatred and confusion. Anniversaries and special occasions that used to be wonderful are now nothing but a sad, empty memory of the past. You think you'll pull out all the roots, but it's not that simple. Pictures have to be destroyed; gifts have to be discarded; and more relationships than you ever dreamed will be broken. And where there are children, the constant Ping-Pong back and forth of their visitation rights go on and on even into adulthood.

What about funerals and weddings? These are strongly affected by a divorce, especially where there are children.

Think of your child's graduation from high school. Everything that has to do with the family is adversely effected by the divorce and brings a constant reminder of the pain and failure. How much better to forgive and make up, and let God restore.

6. Causes Others to Sin by Taking Sides:

Now I beseech you, brethren, by the name of our Lord Jesus Christ, that ye all speak the same thing, and that there be no divisions among you; but that ye be perfectly joined together in the same mind and in the same judgment.
(1 Corinthians 1:10)

If ye have bitter envying and strife in your hearts, glory not, and lie not against the truth.
This wisdom descendeth not from above, but is earthly, sensual, devilish,
For where envying and strife is, there is confusion and every evil work.
But the wisdom that is from above is first pure, then peaceable, gentle, and easy to be intreated, full of

mercy and good fruits, without partiality, and without hypocrisy.

(James 3:14-17)

Not only is the family wounded and fractured, but lifelong friends are put into a strain, and are usually forced to take sides. This increases bitterness and strife which God abhors.

Because God hates division, He abhors divorce:

For the Lord, the God of Israel, saith that he hateth putting away; for one covereth violence with his garment, saith the Lord of hosts: therefore, take heed to your spirit, that ye deal not treacherously.
(Malachi 2:16)

7. Exposes the Family to Greater Temptations:

For the unbelieving husband is sanctified by the wife, and the unbelieving wife is sanctified by the husband: else were your children unclean, but now are they holy.

For what knowest thou, O wife, whether thou shalt save thy husband? or how knowest thou, O man, whether thou shalt save thy wife?
(1 Corinthians 7:14,16)

Not only are there immediate temptations that result from divorce for both mates, temptations increase in the lives of the children both now and in the future. Statistics show that divorce in the next generation is more common among divorced children. The split is not only in the lives of the two parents, but also in the lives of the children. *He that troubleth his own house shall inherit the wind; and the fool shall be servant to the wise of heart* (Proverbs 11:29).

With only one parent now to be accountable to, the child's life lacks stability. He lacks the strength and support for righteousness that comes from both parents being in agreement. Now he is exposed to two parents who hate each other, disagree with each other, and even in little details of life, the child is torn between what one parent thinks is right or wrong while the other disagrees. This can be devastating to a child's character.

When the children grow up and have problems in their own marriages, instead of trying to work things out, because they've had a poor example before them in their parents' divorce, it is easier for them, too, to cop out. So the temptations and problems are multiplied by the divorce even in the generations to follow.

8. It Balances Guilt With Blame:

After King David's adulterous affair he cried out:

> *Deliver me from blood-guiltiness, O God, thou God of my salvation: and my tongue shall sing aloud of thy righteousness.*
>
> (Psalm 51:14)

Those who go through divorce are constantly torn between feelings of self-doubt and guilt, and the desire to blame themselves or their spouse. This seesawing in the spirit makes them unstable and irritated. Any Christian knows that Scripture has a lot to say about our need to be blameless. Many divorced people have shared with me how they have struggled for years with this guilt/blame syndrome, and still struggle with it even after another marriage. When a spouse blames himself, this soon turns into guilt. Scripture has a lot to say about our being blameless:

*Wherefore, beloved, seeing that ye look for such
things, be diligent that ye may be found of him in peace,
without spot, and blameless.*

(2 Peter 3:14)

*That no man should blame us . . . .
Providing for honest things, not only in the sight
of the Lord, but also in the sight of men.*

(2 Corinthians 8:20-21)

*And these things give in charge, that they may be
blameless.*

*But if any provide not for his own, and specially
for those of his own house, he hath denied the faith, and
is worse than an infidel.*

(1 Timothy 5:7-8)

A tragic result of divorce is that the husband blames
the wife and she blames the husband. When this is done
before the children, pitting one parent against the other, it
tears at their loyalty and brings confusion and pain. Many
divorced children go through life blaming themselves for
their parents' breakup, and they too get caught in the guilt/
blame syndrome. Most children can remember times when
they failed to feed the dog or bring in the paper or to take
out the garbage when they were asked to. And in their
childish way of thinking, they tie this in to their parents'
divorce. Add to this the emotional trauma the parents are
going through, making them impatient with the children,
plus their being absent a lot with a new friend etc., and the
child begins to take the blame and feels guilty for the whole
thing.

The guilt/blame syndrome brings bitterness and
unforgiveness that often take years to cancel out. How much

better it is to deal with problems as they arise, apply God's grace and forgiveness to them, and avoid all this extra pain and confusion.

9. It Damages Their Children's Heritage:

God wants children to be able to say:

> *The Lord is the portion of mine inheritance and of my cup; thou maintainest my lot.*
> *The lines are fallen unto me in pleasant places; yea, I have a goodly heritage.*
> *. . . I shall not be moved.*
>
> (Psalm 16:5-6,8)

A divorce often requires the sale of the home. This disrupts the children's environment, sometimes their schooling, their friends and everything that they have grown up around. On top of that, when a stepparent enters the picture, children battle jealousy, rejection and loneliness. When there is a blended family, war often develops over comparisons, partiality and blame, and things go from bad to worse.

The heritage that God had planned for these beautiful children in the beginning is diminished and often destroyed because of the confusion and pain of the divorce. Now, instead of honoring their parents as the Scriptures command, and holding both Mother and Dad up as their models, this heritage is lost, and they are constantly drawn into arguments about comparing, blaming and guilt.

God wants children to be secure with a sense of totally belonging to both parents. But in a divorce, this security is lost. Instead they are pulled first one way and then another. They grow up with a sense of not being sure of who was right and who was wrong, which leads to their not being sure about what is truly right and what is truly wrong.

Instead of this kind of confusion, God has ordained that parents guide their children to God's purposed goal for their lives. This is the result of both parents sticking it out and hanging in there even when things are tough. It makes the home a happy place, as David described in Psalm 127:3-5:

> *Lo, children are an heritage of the Lord: and the fruit of the womb is his reward.*
> *As arrows are in the hand of a mighty man; so are children of the youth.*
> *Happy is the man that hath his quiver full of them:*
> *. . . they shall speak with the enemies in the gate.*

The heritage that God has planned is that children obey and honor their parents, and being trained by them, they will be such mature adults, that when enemies come to the gates, they will be well able to handle them, as it says in Isaiah 54:17:

> *No weapon that is formed against thee shall prosper; and every tongue that shall rise against thee in judgment thou shalt condemn. This is the heritage of the servants of the Lord, and their righteousness is of me, saith the Lord*

In a divorce, not only do the children lose security and much that has always been familiar, they lose continuity and the stability of living with two parents to whom they know that they totally belong forever. Friends may come and go, but the family is for always. This is how God planned it, and it is tragic when it is aborted by divorce.

153

For those who have already experienced divorce, there is no looking back. God can still restore your marriage, unless one of you has remarried. The Lord is expert in the business of restoration, and the only thing that can prevent it is when one of the parties has remarried.

Someone asked me the other day, if there was hope for every marriage. We see twenty-five or more couples a year go back together, and frequently we have the privilege of participating in their wedding. God is faithful, and NOTHING is impossible with Him.

Because of the looseness of the present day, and the immorality that is rampant in our culture, this book would not be complete without listing some of the important Scripture references on this subject of divorce:

1.   The Teachings of Jesus:

Matthew 5: 31-32; 19: 6-9;
Mark 10:11-12;
Luke 16:18

2.   The Teachings of Paul:

Romans 7:2-3;
1 Corinthians 5:9-11; 7:10-13, 39

3.   Leaders to be the Husband of One Wife:

1 Timothy 3:2-5, 12;
Titus 1:5-9

4. **Priests to be Selective in Choosing a Mate:**

Leviticus 21:7,13-14; 22:12-13

5. **Marrying a Former Mate is Forbidden:**

Deuteronomy 24:1-4;
Jeremiah 3:1

5. **How God Hates Divorce:**

Malachi 2:14-16

Our society has drifted from God's plan and ideal. It is no wonder that children and young people today are turning to drugs and alcohol, looking for an escape from reality. Most of these Scriptures are seldom taught in the church today, and where they are taught, there is a sense of saying "Everyone's doing it so it must be okay."

Even in Jesus' day, when he taught on divorce in Matthew 19, his disciples challenged Him, saying with that kind of teaching, it is better not to marry (verse 10). To me, His reply answers a lot of questions. He said, *"All men cannot receive this saying, save they to whom it is given"* (verse 11). And then he taught briefly on eunuchs; how some are born eunuchs, some are made eunuchs by men, and some make themselves eunuchs for the sake of the Kingdom of heaven. He then capped it all with *"He that is able to receive it, let him receive it."*

It was as if Jesus laid out the ideal, then left it to us to choose how much of the ideal we are able to apply personally. The trouble with society is we often make things so markedly black or white, we put everyone into hell who doesn't measure up to the ideal. Jesus didn't do that; He gave us the ideal and left it up to us to choose.

What we must remember is, in all things we are better off when we choose God's highest plan. If you have already gone through a divorce, then begin where you are. Ask God to lead you in this area of your life and don't be impatient or in a hurry. He has your life in His sights, and He will do for you and yours what is always for your ultimate good.